Pieces

A True Story of Assault, Survival, and Empowerment

Lori Luck

PP
Patchwork Press

Pieces

A True Story of Assault, Survival, and Empowerment

Lori Luck

FIRST EDITION

Paperback ISBN: 978-1-0693092-0-4
eBook ISBN: 978-1-0693092-1-1

Copyright © 2025, Lori Luck

All Rights Reserved

No part of this book may be reproduced or transmitted in any form or by any means without the written permission of the publisher.

PP
Patchwork Press

Introduction

"One day you will tell your story of how you overcame what you went through, and it will be someone else's survival guide."
— Brené Brown

HAVE YOU EVER QUESTIONED your existence? Why you were born? Why you're the person you are? Why you feel different from everyone else? I have. I've never felt pressured to conform—or had the desire to. But I've always felt different, always been the "why" girl, questioning everything and longing for answers.

My search for the meaning and purpose of my life has often been answered by service to others. I never feel more needed, or at my best, than when I am helping someone. Anyone.

Not long ago, it occurred to me that maybe I could help others through the story of my journey. That realization set me on a new journey: writing the book you now hold in your hands.

At times in my life, as you will read, I have felt myself to not be whole. To be in pieces. But the title of this book refers to more than just a personal fracturing. Though individually we might all feel at times as though we're in pieces, we must never forget that we are each also a whole piece—a piece of a larger picture, each with a contribution to make to the grand puzzle, no matter how trivial we might at times feel that contribution is.

I hope I can contribute something with the story you are about to read. It has not been easy. It's always painful to revisit old hurts. But in writing this book, I have come to realize the importance of healing those old wounds. It's been a hard emotional journey, but I have come to accept my past. And I have tried my best to forgive.

I didn't have the best examples or role models growing up, but I've become determined to not allow that to stop me from being a good example myself, even a role model, in so far as I can show people what might be possible for them. Like healing. Like forgiveness. Like knowing one's true worth.

I hope my journey helps you see that no matter how fractured you feel, you are still part of something greater. You matter.

Chapter 1
Sylvia

THE WHOLE EVENING SEEMED off. I was only ten years old, but I had an uncanny sense that things weren't right. Not a premonition, exactly. There would be times in my life when I would get premonitions, or something like premonitions, but on this night, what I experienced was more like an unsettling feeling of apprehension. A sense of unattached anxiety. Or maybe this was a feeling I attached to the evening only afterwards. It's hard to say.

For sure, Fred was acting differently. That much was clear. Fred was the adopted son of my brother's godparents. We were visiting their home that evening, not an unusual occurrence. It was my brother David, who was fifteen, my parents, and me. It was after dinner, and the adults were upstairs and David and Fred and I were in the finished basement, sitting on the couch in the rec room, watching TV. The basement was Fred's domain; his bed was down there too. His old bedroom was upstairs, but now, at the age of twenty, Fred needed more space, and I suppose the basement was something like an apartment for him, giving him some independence, or at least as much independence as you can get while still living with your parents.

We were watching *Little House on the Prairie* that evening, an episode called "Sylvia" that registers with viewers of the show even today. *Little House* often took on topics that were controversial, including this particular two-part, 1981 episode about rape. Sylvia was a girl who developed faster than her classmates, leading to some leering from the boys in school. "She's a *lot* more mature than you," Fred told me on the couch that evening. "You're just a little kid." He made other derogatory comments to make me feel small. David, as usual, said nothing in my defence, and I just sat there and took it, confused by Fred's behavior because he'd never been rude or disrespectful to me before.

In any event, the episode included a masked man raping Sylvia in the woods. I was too young to know exactly what happened to Sylvia, but I knew it was bad. When Sylvia's father discovers his daughter has been raped, he tells her not to ever tell anyone, that no one must ever learn of this "disgrace."

I would remember that line.

After *Little House*, Fred suggested a game, but I can't recall which one. Monopoly? Life? Pictionary? "David," he said, "go up to my old room and get it." Whatever the game was, I realized later that Fred didn't have it. The errand was a ruse to get my brother out of the basement, to keep him occupied upstairs looking through Fred's old bedroom for a game that wasn't there.

The ruse worked. David left and Fred immediately locked the door. And then it was just him and me, alone in the basement.

What happened next happened faster than a ten-year-old could possibly process it. But I now knew what happened to Sylvia. Forty-plus years later, I find I'm still trying to process it. Not the act, necessarily, but the ramifications. Something like that stays with you—it was only a few years ago before I could finally stop recalling the smell of Fred on me that night—and the longer you wait to deal with it, the more it seizes upon you.

For years, I didn't know how to deal with it. I was alone with it. With the memories, with the consequences, with the aftereffects. All alone, like Sylvia, and with parents whose attitude was hurtfully similar to her father's attitude, giving me more than one trauma to heal from. Rape is one thing; silence and inaction are something else.

Chapter 2
Childhood

My parents, both Germans, emigrated from Europe in the mid-1960s. But not together. They would first meet each other in Edmonton, Alberta, Canada—two young people with their birth nationality in common and an apparent attraction to each other. Eventually, they would marry and settle down with two children.

Arthur Siegfried Luck was actually born in Warsaw, Poland, in 1924, but he was of German descent, something that would come to haunt him when he reached the age of seventeen. Two years earlier, Nazi Germany had invaded Poland, touching off World War II. Young German men, even those born in Poland, were conscripted into Hitler's army. Dad had no choice but to serve the Third Reich in a German uniform and fight for the country that had invaded his homeland. At least he was fighting the Soviets, a common enemy of both Germany and Poland. Dad fought until 1943, when he was wounded and captured by the Red Army and sent to a Russian POW camp. He survived the camp, but many prisoners did not.

Dad spoke frequently about those years to anyone who would listen, often telling the same war stories over and over again. It seems to me now that maybe he was somehow trying to relive those terrible moments to process them in some way. Looking back, I recognize the symptoms of post-traumatic stress disorder.

Meta Gertraud Engelhardt, ten years younger than Dad, was born in Bavaria. As a young woman, she worked as a sister with the Evangelical Gemeinde, a protestant community, but became severely ill with Crohn's disease at the age of twenty-five. Then type II diabetes. She took time off from her work, but the sisters of the Gemeinde, impatient for her to return, kept pushing her to resume her duties. Finally, in an act not exactly befitting their faith, the sisters decided to push her out altogether. Her real sister, my aunt Hanna, had emigrated to Canada years before and suggested that Meta come over. She could take care of Hanna's four small children in their Edmonton home, allowing Hanna to resume her work as a registered nurse. With nowhere else to go, Mom agreed.

Dad, meanwhile, was doing his share of wandering, looking to get out of Europe altogether, maybe trying to put the bad memories of the war behind him, even though that ended up being an impossible task. At one point he came over to the United States and spent some time in Montana, where he had a great aunt and some second and third cousins. He farmed a bit, having learned his skills as a boy on his family's farm, but steady work was hard to find. He moved to Michigan for a while, then somehow wandered his way into Canada, where he decided to forget farming and look for something more secure. In Edmonton, he found a job in the city's waterworks department, a blue-collar job in a blue-collar town, and that's where he remained for the rest of his working life.

Arthur and Meta met in 1965 and married in 1967, though the details of their courtship remain a mystery to me. Nine months after the wedding, they had a son, my brother David. I came along in July 1971. Mom was a stay-at-home mom until I reached sixth grade. Then she worked part-time as a health care aide, working with clients in their homes. These were elderly people or people with mobility issues, or sometimes both.

We never had a lot of money, something I wouldn't discover until years later when my parents sent me to a better school in a much nicer neighborhood than the one in which we were living. For the first time, I saw how other kids lived. I felt like a fish out of water, something those other kids would be only too happy to exploit for their amusement.

Our neighborhood was in the inner city, and our neighbors were mostly transient. Nobody seemed to stick around too long, except us. Dad was one of the few who actually owned his own home. Most everyone else rented—small houses, apartments, rooms, by the month, by the week, by the day. It would not surprise me if some of the seedier motels in the area rented out their rooms by the hour.

We lived in a very large Victorian-style house, yellow with a green roof. Dad equipped a few of the upstairs rooms with stoves and refrigerators and rented them out for extra income. One tenant was an older Russian gentleman named George, the previous owner of the home. George remained in the house as a tenant for years.

Another tenant was a man named Metro. My only real memory of Metro involves two other men coming to the house to confront him about some money he owed them. They began beating on him and Dad rushed up to Metro's room and threw punches at the men, knocking them down our long flight of stairs. Only recently did I come to learn from my brother that Metro might have owed these men payment for sexual services rendered. David believes Metro was gay, and maybe even a pedophile. He would often playfully tickle David and always end up around his private parts, making David extraordinarily uncomfortable around him, and at an age when he didn't really understand the significance. Dad and Mom had to have witnessed the tickling, but whether they chose to ignore it or simply didn't understand the significance of the tickling themselves, I can't say.

People sold and took drugs across the street and down the block. One of my first memories is of being roundly scolded by my father for picking up a syringe I found in the street. "Drop that!" he yelled at me, scaring me into letting it fall. "That's very bad! Never pick up a needle. Never, never, never!"

Because of the transient nature of the neighborhood, I was never able to make friends, or at least keep them for long. Even in school. I had one best friend from third through sixth grade, but then she moved away. Not that there weren't a lot of kids around; it's just that they seemed to come and go. I never got close to any of them, providing me with precious little experience in forming relationships with people.

At one point there were seven kids living at the end of the street in a two-storey house rented by their single mother, who was on welfare. Two of them—Wendy and Shera-Lee—belonged to a female gang and were always wearing the gang's trademark silver jackets. They would frequently harass other kids in the neighborhood, including David and his buddies, which I'm sure must have been emasculating for David, even at his young age. Wendy and Shera-Lee's brother Doug, a few years older than me, was a little nicer, and David and I would often ride our bikes with him. Doug came to live with us for a time after one of his sisters fell asleep in her bed with a lit cigarette, creating a fire that almost destroyed the whole house.

There was a fire in the house across from us too. Two kids we used to play with lived there with their parents and four Doberman pinschers. The girl, Gina, was hit by a taxi in front of our home when she was three and spent a week in the hospital. Then came the fire. The house was rendered uninhabitable and the family had to move out and, like so many others that once called the neighborhood home, we never saw them again.

After they moved, the house became a place to crash for squatters and an active spot for criminal activity. One day Doug and I, with a couple of Doug's friends, ventured into the house and discovered pentagrams spray-painted on the walls and a bloody pig's head on the floor. "Devil worshippers," Doug said. I couldn't get out of there fast enough, and I never went back. Eventually, the city had the house demolished.

Another nearby home for transients was the Hecla Block, an historic, three-storey Edwardian-style, red-brick apartment building constructed in 1914. It was a fashionable place to live when it opened, and today, in the semi-gentrified area that was once my neighborhood, it is so again. When we lived there, it had fallen into disrepair and was typically vacant except for the vagrants who made it their home. The walls were graffitied, and many of the windows were either broken or covered by plywood. We would often climb up the back fire escape to the roof, where you could feel a fresh breeze and see for miles, a little oasis of charm in a veritable slum.

If the neighborhood had its problems, things weren't necessarily great inside our home either. I can picture Dad sometimes holding Mom's hand, but those images are few and far between, and from mainly when I was very little. Mostly, I remember the bickering, and there was lots of it. Mom and Dad would argue about seemingly everything. Mom could hold her own, but there was no question as to who was in charge of the house. Dad could be domineering and controlling, keeping Mom in a position that I would recognize firsthand later in life.

David and I didn't get along either, even though I would have loved to have had a big brother I could bond with, a brother who would look out for me. When I got older, I saw such relationships in other families, and I envied them. David seemed incapable of it. And it didn't help my frustration to know that David was the preferred child. He got away with stuff I could never get away with. Our parents were especially strict and overly protective with me, something that would become much worse after the assault.

They were also hypercritical. I could do nothing right. Even simple things like helping to wash the dishes. I used too much soap. I didn't use enough soap. I filled the sink with too much water. I wasn't using enough water. It's hard for me today to remember any praise thrown my way at all.

I found an ally, however, in a close friend of my father's, maybe my father's only close friend. Sigmund Selent, my godfather, was also from Poland and of German descent. I knew him as Uncle Sigmund. I loved it when Uncle Sigmund came around. He never married or had children of his own, but he seemed to understand people and children more than my own parents. He talked with Dad often about their strict parenting. Uncle Sigmund was kind and easygoing, the polar opposite of my mother and father. I'm sure that's why he got along so well with Dad. I never saw them argue. Uncle Sigmund would quietly disengage whenever there was a serious difference of opinion.

Of course, I never had the option of disengaging. I was stuck. Mom and Dad's opinions were rules that I had to live by. But one especially positive thing Dad did for David and me was to make sure, from an early age, that we had bikes to ride. I loved riding my bike—often with David or friends, and often alone. I was not afraid to go long distances by myself. I took different bike paths through various neighborhoods to get to the paths that followed the North Saskatchewan River, paths that went on for miles and miles.

I loved these outings, always curious about what was beyond the next turn or around the next bend. My sense of adventure was lost on my mother, who would often point out how different I was from the rest of the family. "Whose child *are* you?" she'd remark. "Where did you come from? You are so different from your father and me." I knew she was right.

Another interest of mine, a passion, really, was the rescuing of abandoned neighborhood cats. From a very young age, I discovered a place in my heart for the occasional pet cat that a resident would discard into the streets, many times as a result of moving out of the neighborhood and not wanting to take the cat along, or maybe because their cat had given birth to kittens and the owner decided there wasn't room for them all. Or maybe they just didn't want to, or couldn't, take care of their pet any longer. I always had a cat or two, sometimes more, that I would feed and bring into the house in the evenings. They needed me and I needed them. Mom let the cats out during the day while I was at school, but they'd return after I got home. Later, after the assault, I would find that taking care of these strays was more than therapeutic. It's no exaggeration to say that the unconditional love of these animals—being needed by them—helped me survive.

David, who seemed to always be looking for new ways to provoke me, didn't share my love of cats. One in particular used to roam between our house and the house of a nearby older couple. One day the cat was hit by a car. She managed to crawl into some bushes, and I could hear her crying, though I couldn't tell from where. Finally, I found her, dying and in pain. I picked her up carefully, cradled her in my arms, and took her home. Then, not knowing what to do, I went with David to the older couple's house and we left the cat with them. I'm sure now that whatever they did was humane, but that's not what David later told me. He claimed they used a "really big knife to kill it," speaking in the most graphic terms he could. For days, I was mortified by the vision of this couple repeatedly stabbing the cat to death.

My parents didn't care for the extra animals in the house either. We always had a dog that Mom and Dad would have around more or less as a watchdog, but the cats were often too much for them. They'd accept one, maybe two, at a time, knowing how much they meant to me, but any surplus cats were packed up and taken to the local SPCA. Except I didn't know that's what happened to them. I'd come home from school to discover a cat missing, and Mom or Dad would assure me that if it hadn't run away, it must have gone back to its original home, although sometimes they would suggest that maybe the cat had been hit by a car. Either way was devastating to me. I couldn't bear the thought that one of my cats had been killed, and I couldn't bear the thought that one of my cats would leave me. What had I done wrong? Had I not spent enough time with them? Had I not provided them with enough love and attention? Maybe I'd spent too much time on my bike or at school.

Guilt-ridden, I would spend hours searching for a missing cat, on foot and on my bike. I'd call for the cat, listening hopefully, and futilely, for a cry that would allow us to reunite. My parents knew this but never said a word. It would be years before I would learn the truth about where these cats went. David would eventually tell me. And then he took some delight in reminding me that the SPCA keeps unadopted animals for only a limited amount of time before putting them down.

Somehow, however, despite it all, we shared some good times as a family. Dad suffered from rheumatoid arthritis, and every other year we would go to Radium Hot Springs, a scenic one-and-a-half-hour drive from the resort town of Banff, and beautiful Lake

Louise with its turquoise waters, through Kootenay National Park. Dad enjoyed soaking in the natural mineral water beneath the vibrant rock cliffs of Sinclair Canyon. The water did wonders for his arthritis, and we would stay for four or five days. My parents were creatures of habit. Mom would cook breakfast every morning in our motel room's kitchenette, and we'd visit the nearby Smitty's Family Restaurant for every lunch and dinner. On the alternate years, we traveled to Montana to see Dad's relatives. My love of horses came from those trips. Montana is where I learned to ride. The horses were as therapeutic for me as the mineral water at Radium Hot Springs was for Dad.

One time, we went to Europe so that Mom and Dad could visit with relatives over there, but I remember virtually nothing of the trip. I'm told I celebrated my fourth birthday there. We had relatives in Edmonton too, of course—Aunt Hanna, Uncle Vince, and their four children. They'd come to visit us and sometimes we'd go visit them. Those were nice times. Aunt Hanna and Uncle Vince were always warm and welcoming.

And I enjoyed school too, even if the school wasn't in such a great area. I did well. So well that later I'd be sent to that better school, where I'd learn how the other half lived.

Edmonton itself changed during those early years of my life. With a population of around half a million, it had been a relatively unknown northern city. Toronto, Montreal, and Vancouver were destination cities, each with its own unique style and appeal. Ottawa was the capital. If people were unfamiliar with Calgary, to the south of us, they would learn of it in 1988 when the city hosted the Winter Olympic Games. Edmonton was something of the forgotten stepchild, blue collar, lacking in charm or glamour, and with nothing, really, to go out of your way to come see. But before long, our city garnered its own share of attention.

Wayne Gretzky became a household name—not only in hockey-obsessed Canada but the world—playing for the Edmonton Oilers of the National Hockey League. Everyone knew the Great One. Gretzky was to hockey in the 1980s what Jordan would be to basketball a decade later. In the 1981–1982 season, Gretzky set the record for most goals in a single season with ninety-two in just eighty games. And with 120 assists, he became the first NHL player to score over two hundred points in a season. The Gretzky-led Oilers would win the Stanley Cup five times throughout the decade of the '80s.

But before Gretzky, the city became known throughout the country for its football team. The Edmonton Eskimos, today known as the Edmonton Elks, won five consecutive Canadian Football League Grey Cup championships from 1978 through 1982. The 1981 team was the best. They won fourteen games that year, each victory by ten or more points. In the Grey Cup game against the Ottawa Rough Riders, quarterback Warren Moon, who would later go on to have an NFL Hall of Fame career, rallied the team from a 20–1 halftime deficit to a 26–23 victory. With the Oilers on the rise, it wasn't long before we were known as the City of Champions.

The city had another reason to feel especially proud in 1981. On September 15, the West Edmonton Mall opened, the largest indoor mall in the world at the time and today second only to Minnesota's Mall of America. It would have a mini-golf course, a water-park, and even an ice rink that the Oilers would sometimes practice on. Now we had something that made us a bona fide, world-class tourist destination.

It was a big year, 1981. I remember watching that Eskimos comeback. I remember the opening of the mall. I remember hearing about a young Wayne Gretzky. Pierre Trudeau was the prime minister that year. I recall listening to "Betty Davis Eyes" by Kim Carnes, "Tainted Love" by Soft Cell, and "In the Air Tonight" by Phil Collins on the radio.

But while all of this was going on in the outside world, 1981 would mean something else for me. Something grim and terrible and crushing. I was only ten years old, but 1981 was the year my childhood would come to an unexpected end.

Chapter 3
Joyless

I cried as we drove home from my brother's godparents' house. My parents assumed I was just tired. It was late, after all. But what they didn't yet know was that less than an hour before, I'd been struggling against Fred's grip, trying to scream with his hand over my mouth. And now I was struggling to process something that I could not understand or make sense of. At home, I lay down on the living room sofa and continued to cry. I was inconsolable.

I would not leave the sofa. Dad and David went to get ready for bed while Mom continued to ask what was wrong.

"Why are you crying?" she asked. "What on earth is the matter?"

Finally, I told her. "Fred hurt me," I said.

"What do you mean?" she asked. "How did he hurt you?"

I explained what had happened, at least as well as a ten-year-old can explain something that she herself does not comprehend. Mom stood silent for a long moment and then called for Dad, who came out of the bedroom, and I had to explain it all again, giving answers to my parents' questions that ultimately made them realize the extent of the assault. There was only one way to consider the matter. I had been raped.

"What should we do?" Mom asked, looking at Dad, flustered.

Dad paced around the living room. "I don't know," he said, his brow furrowed. "I . . . I don't really know. Maybe call the police?"

"Yes . . . maybe," said Mom. "The police."

"Yes, I guess we should," said Dad, nodding slowly. "But look, maybe we should wait until the morning. It's late. We're all tired. Let's get some sleep and we'll deal with this first thing."

"Lori, do you want to go up to bed?" Mom asked.

My bedroom was upstairs. Mom and Dad's was downstairs, just on the other side of the living room wall. The sofa felt safer. "Can I stay down here?" I asked.

Mom nodded and retrieved a blanket and pillow for me. Then the two went into their room. I could hear their voices through the wall, but I couldn't make out what they were saying.

The next morning came, and the decision was made to forget about calling the police. It was best, my parents decided, to try to forget the whole thing. It had happened, but now it was over. The logical thing was to move on.

I'll never know with absolute certainty why my parents landed on the decision to squelch the rape because we never, ever talked about it again. I imagine they were intent on avoiding any potential stigma. For me, and probably more to the point, for them. Who wants to be known as the parents who let their ten-year-old daughter get raped right under their noses? This was the son of their good friends. People they thought highly enough of to appoint as godparents to their firstborn. Harm against me was a reflection on my parents.

For my part, I knew on some level that more should be done. *Something* should be done. Calling the police seemed entirely appropriate. On another level, I was relieved. I didn't want to have to repeat the story again, especially to a complete stranger. I imagined having to explain all the details to an imposing man in a police uniform, him jotting it all down in his little notebook. And if my parents decided that the matter should be kept quiet, who was I to argue? I was only ten. They were adults, and surely they knew best.

If they never spoke to me about it again, did they speak to their good friends about it? Did they tell them what their adopted son did to me? Maybe. I noticed we saw them in church, but we never visited them again, nor did they visit us. And not long afterwards, Fred moved two hours away to Whitecourt, ostensibly for work. Was this a coincidence?

For three weeks, I slept every night on the living room sofa. It was the only place I felt safe. School was out of the question. I was not ready to face teachers and friends. Eventually, however, Mom insisted I sleep in my own bed *and* return to school. I don't know what my parents told the school as to why I'd been absent. I'm sure it wasn't the truth. But I was not the same girl, and everyone knew it. I was quiet and sullen and joyless. The little girl they knew at school was gone.

One day a volunteer parent, Mrs. Boyko, who had known me since kindergarten, asked me point blank what was wrong. "Lori, you've changed," she said. "What's the matter?" When I didn't say anything, she ventured, "Did your brother do something to you? You can talk to me about it, you know."

"No," I answered, "my brother didn't do anything."

"Well." Then she was quiet for a moment, probably hoping I'd confide in her about whatever the problem was. Finally, after an awkward pause, she said, "If you ever want to talk, I'm here. Okay?"

I told my parents that night what Mrs. Boyko had asked. If there were any thoughts about keeping the incident under wraps before then, those thoughts were solidified at that moment. Mrs. Boyko's guess hit way too close to home. Mom and Dad were facing potential embarrassment.

The problem was, I wasn't getting any better. My melancholy was palpable. The school finally suggested I see a therapist and recommended a psychologist who specialized in anxiety and depression in children. Had they known the root problem, the trauma of a rape, they probably would have recommended someone else, surely a woman. The psychologist was a large Black man. As it happened, he was a former professional football player, a lineman who had played for both the Minnesota Vikings and the Edmonton Eskimos. He smiled and was friendly. I look back now and see a nice man wanting to help. At the time, I found him beyond intimidating. He spoke with a booming voice, saying, "Lori, do you know why you're here?"

I shook my head, unable to talk.

"Well," he continued, "your school and your parents wanted you to come see me and talk to me. Why don't you tell me what's going on?"

But I said nothing, shrugging at the continued questions until our hour was up. I refused to go back. "He's scary," I told Mom, and she understood.

Not long after that, I was sent to a kind of psychology workshop where therapists would engage with groups of patients. My group was six young girls, each of us with our own issues. We met for a half day every Saturday for ten weeks. A therapist would go around the room and have us talk about ourselves to the group. Only one of the girls was talkative. She seemed downright happy, and I wondered why she was even there at all. Whatever the reason, the rest of us were grateful to her for taking the pressure off of us. We didn't want to talk at all. I said nothing about the rape.

Sometimes the staff would leave us alone and we'd do our homework from school or maybe interact with each other. What I didn't know was that they were observing us through strategically placed cameras, something I figured out when one of the therapists approached me one day and said, "Lori, look at your fingers. Why are you doing that to yourself?" I'd been biting my fingernails, down to the finger and beyond, actually drawing blood. But I knew it was nothing I'd been doing when the therapists were in the room. That's when I spotted the spy cameras and knew that they'd been watching us. Feeling betrayed, I was even more quiet after that.

The nail-biting thing was a problem. I wasn't conscious of the extent of it until the therapist spoke to me about it that day. "Look, Lori," she said, taking my hands in hers and inspecting my fingers. "It's every single finger. Skin is missing around the nail beds. It's almost down to the bone. Why are you biting your nails like this?" I looked down at my nails to see what I had been doing, but I had no answer for her.

The nail-biting would continue. For years and years.

Back at Alex Taylor Community School, I tried to get along as best I could, but I felt anxious and often unsafe. I no longer trusted anybody. Worse, I felt as if I had no control over these feelings, making me feel even more anxious. I never spoke up in class, never raised my hand.

Some classes and teachers I liked; others only added to the anxiety. There was Mr. Bell, who was physically abusive to kids in a way a teacher couldn't be today, at least legally. He was verbally abusive too, as was Ms. Cho, the music teacher. I was in Ms. Cho's handbell choir and experienced her perfectionism firsthand. She would react angrily to mistakes, and if we were singing, she'd call out anyone who might have been the slightest bit off-key, making derogatory remarks about them to the whole choir. She'd walk around listening for the off-key voices, and sometimes I'd only pretend to sing as she passed by me so that she wouldn't chastise me in front of everyone. I could not have handled it.

Later I would learn about Ms. Cho's background. Born in China, she traveled to Hong Kong during the Second World War. She was exceptionally gifted musically, and after the war she studied music in Toronto, London, and Italy before finally moving to Edmonton to teach. She cared deeply for music and brought in flutes, bells, recorders, cymbals, an abundance of ukeleles, and even costumes for dance, all of which, she frequently pointed out, was expensive and bought and paid for by her. "If I wasn't here," she would say, "you kids would have none of this. I hope you appreciate it. If I ever leave, I'm taking it all with me." Every year we would put on a huge Chinese New Year's performance that would frequently attract important people from the community, including the mayor. Ms. Cho's talents and love of music were admirable, but her drive for perfection perhaps wasn't the best fit for elementary school children.

I liked and admired the principal. Principal Steve Ramsankar was ahead of his time and would go on to receive national recognition for his approach to running our inner-city school. Among other projects, he instituted a nutrition program, a police liaison program, and even an in-school childcare center. The Alex Taylor model would later be promoted to the province of Alberta as the Open and Caring Schools Project, with Ramsankar himself visiting other schools and leading the promotion.

I remember him greeting each student when they came in, sometimes with a hug. He smiled easily and I never saw him angry. He spoke of trying to create a more loving environment in the school and a safe place for kids of all ethnicities, something especially relevant for our school since it was so diverse. Ramsankar himself was from Trinidad.

On Thursdays he held assemblies with different speakers—motivational speakers or sometimes just interesting or popular people from around the area. Sometimes we'd sing songs. The assemblies always opened with everyone standing at attention and singing "O Canada," and closed with everyone standing and singing "God Save the Queen." The teachers would walk around making sure we were all singing respectfully and that there was no talking or fidgeting. This stuck with me, and even today it irks me when I see people not paying attention to the national anthem at sporting events.

But for all of Principal Ramsankar's promotion of a loving, open, caring school, I didn't often see those things reflected in the teachers. Mr. Bell and Ms. Cho and others weren't exactly standard-bearers for Ramsankar's philosophy. But Ramsankar himself was; it was he who took the greatest interest in me, noticing the change in my personality and recommending the ex-football-player therapist, a well-meaning, caring, completely appropriate action to take. How could he have known how I'd react? Maybe he saw the therapist as a big, gregarious, teddy-bear type.

When that didn't work and ten weeks of the after-school workshop didn't help, Principal Ramsankar arranged for something else—a trip to Trinidad and Tobago as part of a foreign exchange program. He still had connections there. Trinidad's Naparima College was his alma mater, and he was able to arrange host families for us to stay with. There were six of us selected, and for the longest time, I assumed it had to do with my grades. Looking back, I can see that Principal Ramsankar chose me as one of the six because his instincts probably told him that I could use a fresh start somewhere, a new and different environment, or at last a chance to get away from where I was. Those instincts were more correct than he could possibly have known.

Chapter 4
Escape

I DIDN'T WANT TO go to Trinidad and Tobago. For all my sense of adventure, and my real yet consciously unrecognized need to be somewhere else, the thought of going so far away and for such a long time—ten months—was scary to me. Whatever was going through my head at the time, and no matter how I felt about my life, I wanted the comfort of familiarity. I wanted routine and normalcy. Maybe if I'd had close friends who'd also been chosen to go, I would have felt better about it, but I barely knew any of the other kids going.

My parents decided the trip would be good for me, though whether the school had to convince them of that, I never knew. Either way, I was angry at them for approving the trip, telling them that if they sent me, I wouldn't call them even once the whole time.

Of course they didn't believe me. As to any concerns they might have had about my safety, if they had any at all, no doubt the school assured them that I'd be well taken care of. After all, the host families were all members of the San Fernando church that Principal Ramsankar had attended when he lived there.

Unlike the other host families, however, my host family did not live in the city of San Fernando. My host family lived in the rural countryside in a small house that was built on stilts so that it wouldn't flood during the rainy season. You could see the ground below through gaps in the floorboards. There was no phone, no hot water, and parts of the house were open to the elements. It was hot during the day and cold at night.

But I loved it. My apprehensions went away quickly once I arrived. My host parents were warm and friendly and loving, and the simple, humble house on stilts soon seemed charming to me. The father, John, commuted every day to his job in the city, an hour and a half away, while the mother, Cecilia, ran a small local ice cream shop. They had three children—two boys and a girl. Marlon was my age, Michael was a couple of years older, and Stephanie was four. The kids had a bedroom, while I was given a mattress to sleep on that rested just outside the parents' bedroom. With a pet dog, the house was a bit cramped, yet strangely never seemed too crowded to me. Somehow, I'd felt more confined in my own home back in Edmonton with more square footage and only two children.

The school I attended was in the city, and I rode with John and the two boys every morning. It was a strict school with a dress code. The boys all wore pressed white shirts and blue pants, while the girls wore white blouses and blue skirts. The other students who had traveled with me from Alex Taylor Community School were put in different classrooms, so I saw very little of them, which was fine with me because I was making new friends.

Sometimes I wouldn't even go to school. I don't know if Cecilia sensed something in me, maybe a sadness I had brought with me, but there were days when she would tell me that it would be okay if I wanted to skip school and go with her and Stephanie to the ice cream shop. Early in my stay, for a couple of weeks, the boys skipped school too and the whole family went to the island of Tobago.

That's how the people of Alex Taylor lost track of me for a time. Principal Ramsankar and Mr. Bell made the trip down with us, then flew back home. From time to time, they'd return to San Fernando for a day or so to check on us, and on one of those trips, they realized, with a sense of dread, that I was missing. I was not at school, and, of course, there was no way to reach my host family even if we hadn't been in Tobago since John and Cecilia had no phone.

Mr. Bell—physically and verbally abusive Mr. Bell—actually threw his arms around me and hugged me when I eventually showed up in San Fernando. "We didn't know where you were!" he said with great relief.

I would find out later that even though I'd gone missing, nobody had ever said anything about it to my parents. Maybe they didn't want to worry them, but when I returned and told them of the miscommunication, they were more than a little upset that no one had bothered to tell them that their only daughter had not been heard from.

Then again, I hadn't had much communication with them, either. I stayed true to my word of not calling, and for ten months, they never heard from me. This was less out of spite, however, and more out of the fact that calling would have been inconvenient. John had a phone in his office in the city and offered to let me use it a few times, but it just seemed easier not to. I didn't really have much to say to them that would have made the hour and a half trip into the city worthwhile. One of the girls from Alex Taylor, on the other hand, called home daily. Paralyzed by homesickness, she never wanted to hang up the phone, and her conversations were long, running up her host family's phone bills to the point of embarrassment for the school. After a few days with John and Cecilia and their children, I felt no such homesickness and no need to call my parents.

Plus, I was enjoying myself too much. Trinidad was beautiful. Off the coast of Venezuela, the small nation of Trinidad and Tobago—two islands, with Trinidad being the larger, more populous island—is a Caribbean treat: white sand beaches; turquoise-blue waters; lush, green hills; colorful tropical birds; and gently swaying palm trees. I found the people friendly and outgoing. We students even got to participate in their annual carnival, dancing in the streets in vibrant costumes to the rhythms of calypso music and steel drums. It was magical.

And it was a surprisingly safe place. If Marlon and Michael and I wanted to go somewhere, maybe into town, Cecilia would often flag down a passing car and pay them a little something to take us along. This seemed to be the way a lot of people got around in the rural areas of the island, a sort of informal ride-sharing program decades before Uber and Lyft. I could not imagine paying a stranger and getting into their car in our Edmonton neighborhood.

The ten months went by quickly. By the end of my time there, I felt a part of the family. Cecilia said she thought of me as another daughter. John said the same thing. It was the first time I was ever exposed to a loving family. It was a healthy environment where every member of the family was kind and supportive, positive and loving. Being included and feeling as though I was a natural part of that family was meaningful and even therapeutic for me, soothing my very soul.

For almost a year, I could forget what had happened to me; it seemed long ago and far away. I carried it with me, of course, but toward the end of my stay in Trinidad, I felt like my old self again.

Even so, home was home, and a big part of me was glad to be returning to my own family. I left Cecilia and John and their family, and the beauty of Trinidad, with mixed feelings. It didn't take long after being back, however, to realize something bleak and disheartening. Ten months had come and gone, and I'd had a wonderful escape. But I was back in Edmonton now, and nothing about my life had changed.

Chapter 5
Edmonton 90210

I RECEIVED SOME DISTURBING news when I returned to the real world of Edmonton: my cousin Christine had begun dating, of all people, Fred.

They had met before I traveled to Trinidad. Fred showed up at a get-together my parents hosted for the occasion of my brother's confirmation in our church, St. John's Evangelical Lutheran. Fred wasn't there long, and I managed to avoid him entirely, but apparently he had chatted with Christine. While I was in Trinidad, he called her and the two started going out.

This was bad enough, but then it got worse. Shortly after I returned, Christine thought it would be a nice idea for the four of us—David and me, her and Fred—to go out one evening. As much as I wanted to, I couldn't figure out a way to say no. I had no decent excuse and wasn't about to tell anyone why Fred made me so uncomfortable. They took us to the Revival Theatre, a discount movie house that typically played the previous year's hits. *Herbie Goes Bananas* was the featured attraction.

I sat on the end, with Christine between me and Fred, and David on the other side of Fred. I'd never been to a movie theatre before, and becoming absorbed by the antics of a Volkswagen Beetle come to life on the big screen in front of me at least partially distracted me from noticing Fred and Christine holding hands. Afterwards, we went to a McDonalds, again another first for me. Our parents never took us out to eat, even fast food. We made bland conversation about the movie, and I said practically nothing the whole time. Finally, mercifully, the evening ended.

Looking back, it's easy to see that the evening was probably not Christine's idea but Fred's—his way of feeling things out, of trying to gauge my level of animosity towards him. Maybe he hoped I'd somehow forgotten the incident in his basement, or at least moved past it. As if a person could do either. No doubt Fred was scared that I would tell someone.

In any event, not long after that, Christine stopped seeing Fred. "He drinks and smokes too much," she said. When he moved to Whitecourt, I could at least feel safe from seeing him again, but of course it wasn't as if Fred would ever really leave my mind, no matter where either of us would eventually move.

Meanwhile, life in Edmonton went on. But one day, something would happen that would have a profound effect on my worldview from that time onward. As a family, we went to the Lutheran church every Sunday. I was baptized there, went to Sunday school there, and, like David, was confirmed there. Religion was a part of our lives. And yet I would not have described myself as spiritual and would not have thought in terms of having a relationship with God or otherwise felt any kind of connection with anything divine. It's something I never thought about. Church was more or less an obligation.

One day I walked with Melody, a neighborhood friend a year younger than I was, to a five-and-dime store a half mile or so from where we started at the Hecla Block. A block or two into our journey, I heard a distinct voice that I took—and still take—to be the unmistakable voice of God, telling me not to look back but to continue directly to the safety of the store. I was made to understand that there were two men following us. At the store, one would wait for us on the corner, the other would wait in the alley.

I glanced behind us, even though I'd been instructed not to, and sure enough, there were two young men, probably seventeen or eighteen, following us. They had apparently come from the Hecla Block too and were staying far enough back to appear as if they were not coming after us, but I now knew otherwise. I felt my pulse quicken and picked up the pace. Melody and I made it to the little store, where we bought the Archie Bubble Gum we'd come for. Then I told Melody that I had seen two men following us and that we should stick around the store for a bit. I didn't mention the voice. Would she have believed me?

After a couple of minutes, I poked my head out the door and sure enough, one of the guys was standing on the corner. Melody and I made a run for it around the far corner of the store but stopped once we hit the alley entrance way. I peered down the alley and there was the other young man, waiting for us just as

I'd been told, looking toward his friend on the street corner.

We took off, crossing the alley behind him while he waited for us to appear from the other direction. We ran a couple of blocks the other way, crossed a busy street, and then cut back again. Looking down the street, now some way from the store, we could see both guys. The one blocking the alley spotted us and yelled back to his friend on the corner. Melody and I didn't wait around. We ran all the way home, zigzagging down different streets. The young men lost us, and I never saw them again.

From that time on, although I would never again hear that voice the same way I'd heard it that day, I would always have a sense that I was never alone. There was somebody there. The universe was not an empty, lonely place. There was a higher power, and that higher power was never far from me.

Something similar happened on a bike ride not long afterwards. I'd been riding in the river valley by myself and was heading home. It was getting towards dusk and about fifty feet ahead of me, standing to the side of the bike path, was a tall, lanky man, maybe in his mid to late twenties. He was staring into the trees and bushes, and I was immediately hit with a sense of apprehension—not quite fear, but an instinctive feeling that the man was dangerous—and it was very clear to me that I needed to avoid him.

I stopped my bike and looked around. The river was on one side of me, a hill ran along the other side, and there was nothing but the tall, lanky man in front of me. I got off the bike and began pushing it up the hill, driving with my legs as hard as I could, feeling the burn in my thighs, and finally making it to the top, where a sidewalk ran alongside a busy road. I stopped to catch my breath, then glanced behind me in horror to see that the man was running up the hill towards me. I jumped back on the bike and pedaled for all I was worth, oblivious now to the burn and not looking back until I was almost home. The man had probably given up the chase as soon as I started riding, but I took no chances.

It wasn't a voice that time, but I felt the same sense of assurance that I was being looked after. And I would feel that instinctive sense repeatedly in my life. But sometimes it presented more questions for me than answers. Where was that sense on the night that Fred raped me? Where was the voice telling me to get out of that basement? Where was God then?

The year after my trip to Trinidad was when I entered junior high, and my parents sent me to Hardisty, a school located in a white-collar, upper-class neighborhood. It was Mr. Bell's idea. He had taught at Hardisty at one time and raved about it. It was supposedly a much better school than the other junior high schools, the schools that were closer to our neighborhood, the schools my friends from Alex Taylor were going to. My grades were worthy of Hardisty, and the school would be a much better fit, more appropriate for my potential. At least that was the thinking, and my parents went along with it.

I hated Hardisty.

The kids were all white, something I wasn't used to seeing. Even though I was white, the uniformity seemed strange, even discomforting. And they all came from money. Lots of money. They belonged to exclusive cliques and despised outsiders. I was unwelcome from the first day. Worse, I was bullied. My neighborhood might have been rough, but I'd never experienced bullies like what I found at Hardisty. When it came to lack of decency and civility, Hardisty's rich white kids were ten times worse than the people I had been used to interacting with. They could be cruel. They ridiculed my clothes, which clearly weren't the designer clothes they all wore. I kept my hair in a ponytail most of the time and they called me tomboy. They made fun of where I came from. I wasn't like them, and my parents weren't like theirs, and they never stopped reminding me of that.

I would spend two years at Hardisty and not make a single friend.

In homeroom one morning, Geri, the girl whose desk was next to mine, asked me what I was going to do after high school. We were in junior high. I hadn't given the matter a whole lot of thought. "After high school" seemed a million years into the future.

"I don't know," I said. "Maybe travel? Then I guess I'll probably go to a tech school or maybe community college."

Geri looked mortified. "You aren't going to university?" But behind the appalled look, there was the hint of a smug grin.

"I don't know," I repeated, feeling my face get warm. "I mean, maybe. I . . . I don't know."

Geri was quick to get up from her desk and share our conversation with her cohorts a few rows away, a couple of whom felt the need to follow up with an interrogation of their own. "You're *really* not going to university?" they asked incredulously. They seemed half amused and half put off, even disgusted. I didn't understand why they were so invested in my life, and I immediately wished I had lied to Geri from the start.

My experience at Hardisty led to years of me worrying about what others thought of me, always keeping me on guard for how I should, and shouldn't, answer questions that were put to me about my life. How I should act. How I should react. What expression I should wear, not to mention what outfit.

It also made me more resentful about my family. Hardisty kids had money, designer clothes, and bright futures. All of that was bad enough in comparison to what I had. But for the most part, they also had tight families. The kids—sure, many of them spoiled—were at least listened to by their parents. They got along with their siblings. They were supported and encouraged.

The resentment kept building up on top of the bullying. For two years, five days a week, it was a barrage of scorn and harassment from the students at Hardisty. And for two years, almost daily, I pleaded with my parents to take me out of that school. For two years they didn't listen to my pleas. Years later I would look back at my childhood and think about the parallels between the rape and the bullying—the double victimizations. First at the hands, respectively, of Fred and the Hardisty rich kids, and then at the hands of my parents who, in both cases, did nothing.

Eventually, my parents were worn down by my complaining and relented on the Hardisty question. But their response was to take me from one extreme to the other. If I didn't care for the school in the rich neighborhood, they'd send me to a school in a poor neighborhood, poorer than ours even. And so I found myself walking one-and-a-half kilometers each morning to McCauley Junior High School in the inner city.

The school itself was fine, and I could even handle the neighborhood. But hardly a day would go by that I wasn't approached, walking to school, by some man in a car asking if I wanted a ride. Our church happened to be not too far from the school, and so the first couple of times, I naively assumed it must have been a fellow parishioner looking to do a good deed. But when I'd get close and couldn't recognize them, my instincts would kick in again.

Sometimes the driver would circle the block and try a second time to get me in the car. "Are you sure you don't need a ride?" The men were typically dressed in business suits and drove nice cars. Later I would realize they were on their way from the suburbs—from the supposed "better" neighborhoods—to the downtown corporate area where they most likely worked. I knew that a couple of blocks over, it was not uncommon to see prostitutes walking the streets, but there I was, no more than a kid, hurrying to school with my backpack slung over my shoulder. This was no case of mistaken identity. One morning a guy in a not-so-nice vehicle, and not in a suit, dispensed entirely with the pretense of wanting to give me a ride, giving me instead a toothless smile and waving a wad of cash.

But I made friends at McCauley, a mix of acquaintances from a diverse student body. I felt comfortable there. Nobody bullied me. And even with the disturbing drivers trying to pick me up and the rough neighborhood, I received a decent education at McCauley. And a much more valuable one than what I got at Hardisty—a better school, maybe, for book learning, but in other ways a vastly inferior place.

Chapter 6
No Way Out

A HIGHLIGHT OF MCCAULEY Junior High School for me was the ninth-grade play. We did *The Glass Menagerie* by Tennessee Williams, the play that launched his famed career, a lot of it autobiographical in nature. Our drama teacher thought I might be good for the part of Laura Wingfield, the main female lead, a character with a disability and an inferiority complex. Also trying out was Charmaine Rose, a girl who was outgoing and charismatic. I was floored when the teacher chose me. "You nailed it," she said to me after the audition. "I just had to choose you."

I hungered for praise, and the teacher's words stick with me to this day. Approval and recognition were in short supply for me. I never received either at home. The teacher's confidence meant the world to me, and I worked extra hard, not wanting to let her down.

We rehearsed for days, performed for the entire school, and then did an evening performance for family members. During our curtain call, listening to the applause, I felt transported. The whole experience was exhilarating. The applause and the drama teacher's praise gave me reasons to feel good about myself. Graduating from McCauley, I felt a pull towards theatre and decided to make the Victoria School of Performing and Visual Arts the place where I would spend my high school years.

In tenth grade, however, as strong as the school's theatre program was, I took a slight detour from drama to physical education. The school offered a new kind of acrobatic cheerleading, headed by a passionate teacher named Diane Greenough. I was intrigued and decided to give it a try. Ms. Greenough had been hired by Bob Dean, the principal, who was famous in Canadian Football League history, and legendary in Edmonton, for kicking the convert for the game-winning point for the Eskimos in the 1954 Grey Cup. I admired Ms. Greenough's positivity, and through her, we all learned responsibility, punctuality, teamwork, commitment, and leadership. She also taught two psychology classes, which I loved.

Cheerleading resonated with me. At home I would watch *Solid Gold*, a TV show that played the top hits of the time, with the Solid Gold Dancers performing choreographed routines in glitzy costumes. I couldn't take my eyes off the screen. I loved the coordinated movements of the dancers, and I saw that same kind of action in cheerleading. I eventually made the cheer team and enjoyed every moment of it.

We're for the red; we're for the white; we're for the team that's got the fight! Yaaaay, Vic!

So talented was Dianne Greenough that she would later go on to coach the Edmonton Eskimos cheer team.

But at home there remained little to cheer about. The strictness I experienced as a child only became worse through my high school years. I couldn't go out, even with friends my parents knew. Religiously devout, Mom and Dad feared the perils of the outside world for me and didn't trust my teenage judgment. I had to be in early every evening, weekends included. My parents were worried about boys, they were worried about alcohol, they were worried about drugs. Keeping me home was the only way to protect me from all these evils. And neither Dad nor Mom was shy about using physical punishment if they felt the situation required it. Dad used a strap, while Mom's preference was a wooden spoon.

David, as always, could come and go as he pleased. He had few, if any, restrictions. Boys, apparently, weren't subject to the same temptations, or at least the repercussions weren't as severe. Boys couldn't get pregnant, which, of course, was the biggest fear of all. It didn't help that a cousin—Christine's older sister—had become pregnant as a teenager a few years before I entered high school. In the days when this was considered shameful, she was sent off for a few months to a school for unwed mothers, then returned home after giving up her baby for adoption. No doubt, this was on my parents' minds, but it was a family secret that they withheld from me. You didn't talk about this kind of stuff back then. You swept it under the rug. I wouldn't learn of my cousin's pregnancy until I was in my thirties.

My parents' favoritism of David was always on display. He was the firstborn, and he was way more like them than I would ever be. "David wouldn't do that," I would always hear. "Why can't you be more like your brother?"

Sometimes, but not often, the strictness was even too much for my mother. I would plead with her to let me go out with my friends, knowing that any such plea to my father would fall on deaf ears. "Mom," I would beg, "if I can't ever go out, I'm never going to have any friends! I'll have no social life at all!" She'd make me promise to come home at a reasonable hour and then look the other way as I snuck out while Dad sat in the living room watching TV, never the wiser.

The idea of losing friends was real. A couple of girlfriends came over to the house one Saturday night on their way to another house where a girl was hosting an innocent sleepover. Not content to prevent me from going, my parents took it upon themselves to monitor my friends' movements too. "Oh no, you're not going out," Dad told them. "You can stay here and have fun here. You can even sleep over here tonight if you'd like."

"But our friend is expecting us," one of the girls said.

"Well, it's too late for respectable girls to be going out now," my dad argued. "Look at the time."

"But our parents said it was okay. We're allowed to!"

"Well, your parents aren't here," said Dad. Then, pointing towards Mom, he added, "We're the parents in this house. You'll listen to us now."

My friends were near tears. Eventually, my dad relented, but the incident was beyond humiliating for me. The next time I saw the girls, all I could do was just sheepishly grin and say, "Sorry about my dad."

Good old Uncle Sigmund would continue to try to help me by taking my parents aside and letting them know they should give me more latitude. "Lori's a good girl," he would tell them. "You're much too strict."

"Easy for you to say," my parents would tell him, immediately defensive. "You don't have any children!"

"Sure, but I was young once," Uncle Sigmund would say. "And I know how important it is for a young person to be able to go out with their friends and enjoy a little freedom. Plus, she needs to learn how to be responsible for herself. How can she do that with you supervising her every move?"

"I think we know how to raise our own kids!" my parents would huff, voices rising. "Lori is *our* daughter!"

True to form, Uncle Sigmund would back down, throwing me a little shrug as if to say, "I tried, kid."

Deep within, something started to bubble towards the surface in those days. From time to time, my mind would go back to the rape and my parents' response, or lack of response, to it. I couldn't help but replay in my mind the reaction they had when I told them of Mrs. Boyko's question to me after I'd finally returned to school: "Lori, did your brother do something to you?" I could now see that my parents' concern at that moment was about the perception of their parenting and David's behavior. Mrs. Boyko's concern was for *me*. She showed me what care and concern looked like. She said genuine, loving things to me. She acted, in short, the way my parents should have acted. The way they didn't act. I tried not to think about it, but it was impossible to let it go. And I was still angry from the two years they had forced me to go to Hardisty.

Things got worse. My parents' control of my life didn't stop with high school. After graduation, they mapped out my immediate future. I was to go to university. I didn't know exactly what I wanted to do, but I had thoughts of pursuing some sort of career in social work. I wanted to help people. Mom promptly shot that idea down. "That's not a good career for a young woman," she said. "You'd have to work evenings and weekends."

Instead, they thought a career in education would be good for me. Why? Because that's the direction David had gone. David had first acquired a two-year diploma in business administration from Grant MacEwan Community College and then had attended the University of Alberta education program to obtain his Bachelor of Arts. And if that path was good enough for David, certainly it was good enough for me. It would be the University of Alberta education program for me too.

Besides, didn't I understand the role of a daughter? "The reason we had you kids was to take care of us in our old age," Dad told me more than once.

It all came to a head shortly before I entered the university. I wanted to go out one evening with my friends, Diane and Brent, both of whom my parents knew. Diane was cousins with a neighbor friend across the street. Along with Brent, we'd all played together as kids. Mom and Dad had known them for years. And yet, one more time, they didn't trust me to leave the house.

I lost it.

I don't know exactly what I screamed but I unloaded eighteen years of frustration. I screamed about their rules, I screamed about their favoritism towards David, I screamed about their choosing of my career. I even screamed about their attitude toward the rape. I yelled. I cried. I told them I felt like a prisoner. I told them I felt unloved. I told them I felt I didn't even belong in our family.

In between my rantings, they tried to inject denials. David was there and of course he promptly took our parents' side. There was no favoritism; that was my imagination. And they were only looking out for my own good, trying to keep me safe from the evils of the world. And of *course* they loved me. Of *course* I belonged.

I was having none of it. I continued to yell and scream and cry, and soon everything devolved into a shouting match. Finally, I ran out of the house and didn't stop running until I made it to Diane's house.

Diane tried to calm me down as I told her what had happened. I felt shame at the time. That was my initial reaction to what had happened. I should have been able to sit my parents down and have a rational conversation with them. I should not have acted so emotionally. Today I know that a rational conversation would have had no effect on them or on my circumstances, but that night I felt as if I should have been more composed, more stoic, more reserved—as if an eighteen-year-old in my situation could have been any of those things. And as if they didn't deserve every word that I yelled that night.

Besides the shame, I also felt the futility. I knew that my raving made no difference. I would still be living like a prisoner in my own home, and I was still destined to live the life my parents wanted me to live.

There was no way out.

Diane and I talked in her living room and then I excused myself to use the bathroom. I don't know if the thought of what I was about to do next was a conscious one, but I found myself peering into the medicine cabinet. Among the hair products and Band-Aids and toothpaste, I spied a bottle of aspirin and a bottle of sleeping pills. I didn't spend a moment thinking about it; I swallowed a handful of each and then returned to the living room. Diane was talking to me but soon my body started feeling heavy, like I couldn't move. Then I felt as if I were drifting—drifting farther and farther away. Diane's voice faded into the distance until I could barely hear her at all.

And then everything went black.

Chapter 7
Moving On, Moving Out

I AWOKE IN THE hospital, disoriented and sick. Diane had called an ambulance after I had lost consciousness. In the emergency room, they gave me activated charcoal to drink. Activated charcoal binds to whatever a person ingests, reducing its absorption, but the charcoal had a gritty taste that made me vomit. Of course, this worked just as well to rid my body of the pills I had swallowed.

As I recovered, with Diane sitting in the waiting room with Brent, who had shown up by then, a nurse took it upon herself to give me a lecture. "Do you know that your friends are out there crying? Have you even for a second thought about them? Do you realize that your selfish actions have put them through *hell*? You should be ashamed of yourself, young lady. You've been very selfish. You're lucky to have friends like that." Then, shaking her head, she said, "Now, do you *still* feel like dying?"

I didn't answer. What I wanted to tell her was that if I ever did feel like dying and I attempted suicide again, I'd do it right so that I wouldn't have to be subjected to a cold-hearted lecture from a cold-hearted nurse.

The staff on the psychiatric floor, where I was subsequently sent for three days, was much nicer. The main nurse was young and friendly and related easily to the patients. She told me she enjoyed working on the floor because she could wear her own clothes, not the white uniforms that nurses in other areas of the hospital had to wear. The doctors—mostly psychiatrists—were all pleasant and approachable too. They tried to get me to open up about my life, but I didn't say much. Dad and David came to visit me, but the visit was awkward and stilted. Mom stayed home.

At the end of the first day, I asked an intern what it would take to get me out of the hospital.

"Well," he said, "the doctors just need to make sure you're not a risk to hurt yourself again. That's the main thing."

From then on, I told the doctors what I knew they wanted to hear, and two days later, I was released.

Back home, things remained the same. We all fell back to the default position of ignoring the elephant in the room. Nobody talked about the suicide attempt, just as nobody had talked about the rape eight years before.

The psychiatrists at the hospital had recommended follow-up therapy, but my parents must have declined the recommendation because I never saw anyone after the hospital stay. Did they think I was okay? Did they imagine my depression had just been some passing phase? Truthfully, I hadn't committed to not attempting suicide again. In fact, suicidal thoughts would be with me from time to time throughout my life. Dark moments when all I wanted to do was end the pain and anxiety.

What kept me from trying at the time was the thought of again failing. I'd read stories of people who had jumped from buildings only to survive with broken legs or broken backs. Or people who'd taken pills to end it all but wound up in comas or, worse, mentally disabled for the rest of their lives, dependent on others to feed them and help them use the bathroom. One story I read was of a man who tried to shoot himself in the head. At the last second, he flinched. A straight-on shot would have killed him. This one spared his life but did massive brain damage. What if that happened to me? Worse, I was sure that the same nurse would be there to lecture me again, to tell me I should be ashamed of myself.

So instead of killing myself, I chose to enroll at the University of Alberta to try to make the best of things. Maybe I wasn't going to do social work, but with a Bachelor of Arts in Education, there was nothing to keep me from helping people. I would do so by teaching, and I decided to pursue my studies with a focus on special education. It felt right. An imperfect human being helping those who needed it most. A good fit.

Before classes started, I moved out of the house. The City of Edmonton offered Dad and a few other homeowners on our street enough money to buy new residences in other areas of Edmonton. The city had plans to demolish some of the homes in our neighborhood to make room for low-income housing. The area was going to be revitalized. The offer came at a good time. My childhood home needed serious repair work. Dad was handy, but he and Mom were getting older, and his arthritis was getting worse. And Mom had talked for years about new appliances. It was 1989, yet she was still using a vintage ringer washing machine.

With the proceeds of the house sale, Mom and Dad bought a new house in a different area, but still within a reasonable distance of the downtown core. It was a smaller place than our big Victorian, but at 1,800 square feet, it was big enough, and everything about it was up to date. Plus, it had four spacious bedrooms. To cap it off, Dad bought Mom a new Maytag washer and dryer set.

It was good timing for me too. With my university classes starting, it seemed like the right time to get out on my own. Mom and Dad preferred that I move into the new house with them, but there was nothing that appealed to me about remaining under their control. This was my chance at freedom. And if I had any doubts at all about moving out, they were put to rest when David claimed the only bedroom I would have wanted—one that was on another level of the house and away from the other bedrooms. By then he had taken a teaching position in Fort Chipewyan, a nine-hour drive north. He would have need of the room only during school holidays, and yet Mom and Dad agreed that the room should permanently be his. That was the final straw.

Besides, I was eighteen now and officially an adult. I'd also saved enough rent money from a summer job I'd taken at a dry-cleaning plant, as long as I found a roommate. I knew I could make it work. I had to. Mom and Dad, on the other hand, were convinced I'd soon be returning home. With school and work, it would all be too much for me to manage.

They didn't care for my choice of roommate either. Cindy was a girl I knew from high school. She was a troubled soul with her own set of issues who had dropped out of school in the eleventh grade. She and I had hung out a few times, and she'd been to our house. The last time she'd come over, Dad had thrown her out. Unbeknownst to me, he had suspected her of stealing change on previous visits from the pocket of his jacket, which hung in the hall closet near the front door. One day, to confirm his suspicions, he planted a five-dollar bill in his jacket pocket. Cindy and I were upstairs in my bedroom, and at one point she excused herself to use the bathroom. But she took a detour first to the hall closet. A few minutes after she returned, Dad stormed into the room.

"Cindy!" he boomed, "thieves are not welcome in this house! Now get out!"

Cindy looked stunned. "Mr. Luck . . . I don't know what—"

Then Dad started screaming about how he had seen her go to the closet. When he'd gone to check his jacket pocket, sure enough the five-dollar bill he had planted was gone.

"I didn't take it!" Cindy declared. "I swear!"

"Empty your pockets!"

Cindy, crying now, did as Dad demanded, and there was the five-dollar bill.

"Lori!" Dad shouted at me, "how can you allow a thief into our house?"

"But it's my five dollars!" Cindy cried. "I had it with me when I came in! I didn't take your money!"

"Cindy, get out and never come back!"

"Don't worry," Cindy shot back, "I won't!" And then she ran down the stairs and out of the house, slamming the door behind her. Part of me felt sorry for her, even though I knew she'd stolen the money. What really hurt was that I came to realize that going through Dad's jacket pockets was the only reason Cindy had come over to see me.

I didn't see her for a long time after that, but during that summer before university, I ran into her one day at the women's clothing store where she worked. We talked for a bit, with her asking at one point, "Does your dad still think I stole his money?"

I nodded.

Cindy mentioned how, like me, she'd like to move out of her parents' house. I told her I needed a roommate, and soon enough we were looking for an apartment together, eventually stumbling across a small, older, two-bedroom bungalow. It wasn't much of a home, but between the two of us, we could just make the rent, and we signed a year-long lease.

Once school started we didn't see much of each other. By then I had left the dry-cleaning plant and had taken a part-time job at a clothing store at the

West Edmonton Mall. Between work and school, I saw Cindy only late at night back at our bungalow. Our conversations were short and generic. It was just as well; we had very little in common. She smoked and drank a lot, and we didn't share any of the same friends. On the rare times we went out together, she'd end up ditching me for some guy she'd meet.

In the meantime, I became involved in something else. Dianne Greenough, the cheerleading teacher from the Victoria School of Performing and Visual Arts was, by then, working with the Edmonton Eskimos Cheer Team, and she invited me to try out. In fact, she encouraged all the cheerleaders from our high school to try out. I made the team as an alternate, performing at three CFL games in my first season. It was fun and a great diversion from work and school. I knew a lot of the other cheerleaders from Victoria, and I loved having Dianne as our coach. We would perform several routines during the games, each one including dancing and acrobatic stunting. We would perform at events around the city too. Like in high school, I was the girl who was tossed into the air.

Around that time I reconnected with my friend Diane, and I also became close with Stephanie. Stephanie was a neighbour, outgoing and fun. She was a free spirit, and I admired her for her easy-going ability to get along with seemingly everyone. One night after work, I met her for coffee. Afterwards, Stephanie drove us home, and we happened to pass a massage parlour on the way. We saw a man enter, and Stephanie slyly smiled. "Want to go in?"

We suspected this was no ordinary massage parlour. This was a parlour that offered "extras."

"Seriously?" I chuckled.

"Sure."

"I don't know . . ."

"C'mon," Stephanie said, pulling the car over to the curb. "Haven't you always wondered about these places? It'll be fun to check it out!"

We both laughed, and I said, "Okay, let's do it."

Inside the parlour was a dimly lit reception room with several girls sitting around a TV that was showing a family sitcom. I noticed cameras in the reception area and at the top of a set of stairs that led to what I assumed were private rooms. The girls were all young, probably anywhere from eighteen to twenty-five, and I was struck by the irony of what they were doing for a living and the wholesomeness of the show they were watching.

I wanted to turn around and leave, but when one of the women rose to greet us, I heard Stephanie say, "We're here about a job." I had to bite my lip to keep from laughing out loud.

"Just a moment," the woman said, and she retreated to a back office.

I shot Stephanie a glance, as if to say, "What are we *doing* here?"

Presently, a tall, slim Black man came out from the back and proceeded to give us a tour of the place. Then he ushered us into his office separately, Stephanie first. When it was my turn, he explained the job responsibilities.

"Now listen," he said, "I get a lot of new customers in here, but there's a lot of regulars too. Those are the ones we really want to take care of. Sometimes my girls don't like everything that's requested of them, but it's always best to do what the client wants. If you've got a problem, you can bring it up to me, but only afterwards, understand? The name of the game is to keep the customers happy and coming back. Ready to start?"

I hemmed and hawed. "Well, you know, my friend is waiting for me out there..."

"Sure, she can start too."

The man didn't seem like the patient kind. He was intent on bringing us on board right then and there. I had to think quickly.

"Well, the problem is, I'm... uh... I'm on my period just now. My friend is too, as a matter of fact. Soooo... maybe it would be best if we came back, you know, in a few days?"

The man looked thoughtful and then slowly nodded. "Okay, how about this Friday?"

"Friday. Sure. Friday."

I left his office, and Stephanie and I made it out to the car before we both exploded in laughter. Going into the massage parlour was the kind of fun lark that only Stephanie would think to do. Later, however, I found myself wondering about those girls. What had brought them there? What circumstances had come about in their lives to land them at the doorstep of a seedy massage parlour? I knew they hadn't entered the place on a lark like us. When they'd come in, they were looking for work. And they were apparently willing to do things they didn't want to do to keep the man's clientele "happy and coming back."

In the meantime, I continued going to school, working part-time, enjoying the occasional stint with the Edmonton Eskimos Cheer Team, and relishing my freedom from home. One night Diane and another friend, Kathleen, invited me out to Cook County Saloon, a country music nightclub. It was free line-dance lesson night. I wasn't necessarily a fan, but I went along. After about an hour of line dancing, we sat down and Diane pointed out a tall, slender guy staring at us. Eventually he came over and asked me to dance. His name was Greg, and we two-stepped around the dance floor for a couple of songs. We went back to the table and chatted for a bit, but it was a Thursday night and I had class the next morning. Greg asked for my phone number on our way out. He seemed nice, and I gave it to him. True to his word, he called me, and he didn't waste any time. I was barely home from Cook County Saloon before my phone rang.

"I really enjoyed meeting you tonight," he said. "Do you want to go out tomorrow night?"

"Well, I can't tomorrow night. I have to work."

"Blow it off," he said. "Call in sick or something."

"I really can't," I said. "They need me."

"Oh, come on. You can miss one night. They'll get along okay without you."

He kept insisting, I kept telling him Friday night was no good, and we finally settled on going out Saturday. His insistence had seemed kind of charming at the time, and I would never have considered it a red flag. But with Greg, there would be plenty more red flags to come.

Chapter 8
Greg

GREG AND I MET for a late coffee Saturday afternoon, followed by dinner at a nearby restaurant. I was surprised to learn he was seven years my senior. He looked younger to me, no more than maybe twenty-one. He worked for the Workers Compensation Board of Alberta and had recently moved out of his parents' house. Now he was living with his brother.

We talked about our dating histories. Neither of us had dated much and neither of us had been in a relationship. Greg seemed relieved to hear this about me. For my part, I was left to wonder why a guy his age hadn't ever had a girlfriend. It was another red flag that I missed. His explanation—his education had been very important to him, and after university he had traveled a lot, including six months in and around Fiji—seemed to make sense. "Plus," he added, "I guess maybe I can be a little picky about who I spend my time with."

We started seeing each other regularly. In short order, I discovered Greg had a domineering personality and an apparent need to be in control. But I liked the attention he gave me; I hadn't gotten much attention from men before, and I was flattered by it. Besides, Greg was older, and I was inexperienced in relationships. Of course, so was he, but I didn't allow that to matter at the time, and it wasn't hard for him to take charge. I let him, imagining that he knew best and thinking it was normal. My role models were my parents, after all. And Dad was always in charge.

My friends, however, could see what I could not. In Greg they saw sarcasm, selfishness, and judgementalism. One night Diane and Kathleen and I went back to Cook County Saloon, this time with Greg. I wore a cute black-satin wrangler's jacket with silver lettering on the back. Diane and Kathleen wore the same. In fact, they had encouraged me to buy the jacket so that the three of us matched. All night, Greg criticized the jackets. "You guys look like you belong in a gang," he said. I'm not sure I understood at the time that it was more than about jackets. Greg was jealous. My relationships with my friends were threatening to him. In time he would try hard to keep me from my friends.

From time to time, Diane and Kathleen would talk to me about Greg, voicing their concerns in subtle ways, but I would make excuses for him and tell them that they didn't really know Greg the way I did. In hindsight it's apparent that they knew him even better.

Greg was also threatened by my participation in the Edmonton Eskimos Cheer Team. "You're just doing it for the attention," he'd say. "And I'll bet the players come on to you all the time."

"It's not like that," I'd tell him, struggling at the time to understand why he would take something that was innocent and fulfilling and fun and turn it into something negative. But in the end I gave in. After three years on the cheer team, rather than be continually subjected to Greg's antagonism, I quit.

Things got worse. Greg became verbally abusive over time. And hypercritical. As much as, or more so than, my parents. I let it all slide, maybe because I hadn't really known anything different in my life.

Also, I was caught up in my studies. My interest in education, specifically in teaching kids with disabilities, was growing. During my student teaching, I fell in love with the work. I felt needed, maybe for the first time in my life outside of my rescue cats. I found it stimulating and challenging. These were kids with developmental problems including hearing, visual, speech, or language disabilities. Some had Down syndrome. Several had autism, and a few had been diagnosed with fetal alcohol syndrome.

Each kid had a different learning style, and it was our job to figure it out, to learn how to reach them. Learning could be a frustrating experience for all of them and some had anger issues, but we dealt with each one and found what worked. One student couldn't speak, but we taught him how to talk to us by tapping out his needs. One tap to go to the bathroom, two taps to get a book he wanted. It was gratifying work. I was making a difference in these kids' lives.

During my student teaching, I was given experience in different places and at different levels. One semester I was in an elementary school, another semester I was in a junior high school. For a while I was even assigned to a Catholic school, even though I could never get a permanent position there because I wasn't Catholic. In the public schools at the time, there were separate classrooms for special-needs students, and there were teaching assistants too. The kids received a lot of one-on-one attention. Later, for budgetary reasons, special-needs students would be integrated into regular classrooms, and they would not get nearly the attention they needed. Plus, their presence could be disruptive for the other students. It was a disappointing turn of events, and a lot of the joy would go out of the profession for me at that point. But during my student-teaching days, I enjoyed every moment.

After being together for a couple of years, Greg and I decided to move in together. His mother bought a house for us to live in, and we made the monthly mortgage payments. We talked about marriage. Greg even gave me an engagement ring at one point, but he made it clear that a wedding would have to be down the road. "There's too much going on right now," he would say. Nonetheless, we decided to have a baby, and in my last year at the University of Alberta, I became pregnant.

Two months later Greg got cold feet. He had been on board with the idea, but suddenly it was as if someone had flipped a switch. Or maybe he'd never really been on board. "I can't do it," he told me. "I'm not ready to be responsible for another life."

And then he decided he might not be ready for marriage either. He wanted to separate, to think things through. But of course the house was in his mother's name. Separation meant me leaving, not him.

With nowhere else to go, I reluctantly moved into my parents' house. Five months later, Greg changed his mind again. He'd had time to think about it. "I'm feeling more comfortable with the idea now," he said.

I didn't move back right away. I stayed with my parents, but Greg and I started spending more time together. In April 1993, I gave birth to a girl we named Jessica. It was the same month as graduation. With a baby and a university degree, I finally moved back in with Greg to await the start of the new school year in September. I had a teaching position lined up at an elementary/junior high school. During the summer I was able to spend every moment with Jessica, then Greg's mother babysat her when I went to teach.

At home Greg's domineering personality ruled. I would work all day and then come home to face all the chores of running a household myself. I took care of Jessica, I cooked, I cleaned, I did the grocery shopping. Again, I imagined this dynamic to be normal. This is what all mothers did, wasn't it?

Greg's mom was good with Jessica, but after a year she decided it was too much to babysit her all day and my mom took over. Overall, I got along with Greg's parents, but I found them to be standoffish, sometimes even cold. Not long after Jessica was born, Greg's father became ill with Pick's disease, a form of degenerative dementia. Symptoms include personality changes, speech difficulties, trouble with language, and cognitive problems, all of which become progressively worse. Greg's dad was slipping fast, the main reason his mom could no longer look after Jessica. One time, we were in their home and we witnessed Greg's father shuffling repeatedly around the house, jittery and unable to remain still. Greg's mother sighed impatiently and said, pointing to her husband of over thirty years, "See? This is my life now. Taking care of him."

As for my marriage, Greg's verbal abuse finally started taking what, in retrospect, seems its inevitable course: It turned physical. One evening we were out on a family walk around a nearby pond. It had rained the previous couple of days and the ground was muddy in places. I don't remember what, but I said something that upset Greg. In his anger he shoved me down hard, and I fell into the mud. Jessica was with us, and I tried to remain strong and not cry.

People in a passing car witnessed the incident and pulled over. It was a young couple, and the woman in the passenger seat leaned out of the window and said, "Are you all right?"

"Yes, I'm fine," I said, even as I was trying to wipe the mud off my clothes.

The man behind the wheel was about to take off, but the woman turned to him and said, "No, wait. Hold on." Then she turned back to me. Lowering her voice, she asked, "Are you *sure* you're all right?"

"Yes, thank you," I said, trying my best to sound nonchalant. "I'm fine. Really."

The woman looked unconvinced, but the couple drove off and we walked the few blocks home, me muddy from head to toe.

"Ahh, that felt good," Greg chuckled.

Not long after that evening, we argued about something minor and Greg pushed me up against a wall. By now the red flags were impossible to ignore. And when, a few weeks later, he dragged me down a flight of stairs, I called the police. I was now scared of Greg.

Two officers came to the house and charged him with assault. One of the officers took me aside. "Do you have someplace to go tonight? Family or friends you can stay with? He'll probably make bail, and you shouldn't be here when he comes back."

I took Jessica and went to my parents' house. It was midnight by then. Greg did, in fact, make bail that night and his parents hired what they referred to as a "pit bull" defense attorney. But when Greg's case came up, the pit bull attorney was of little help. Greg was put on probation, forced to attend anger management counseling, and required to perform one hundred hours of community service.

I stayed with my parents, and for months Greg and I had no contact. But as his year of probation wound down, he decided he wanted full custody of Jessica. I knew this was more out of spite than out of any love he felt for our daughter. I hired an attorney and the battle was on. At the final hearing, Greg wasn't helped by the findings of his court-mandated counseling: He'd been diagnosed with narcissistic personality disorder. I received full custody of Jessica, with Greg allowed to have visitation one night a week and every other weekend.

I took some time to read up on narcissistic personality disorder. People with this mental condition have an extra-high sense of their own importance. They seek attention, even admiration, believing themselves worthy. They can be arrogant, thinking that they're superior to those around them. They quickly become envious and resentful of others who garner the attention they feel that they themselves are owed. They lack empathy and cannot recognize the feelings of others. Things always have to go their way. And they are quick to anger.

Greg checked all the boxes. As I read about the condition, it seemed to me that all that was missing was a note that narcissists often like to push people into the mud and drag them down stairways.

But not long after I'd received custody, Greg started reaching out to me, sending me notes of endearment, flowers, even edible arrangements and Cookies by George. He wanted to get back together. He wanted me and Jessica to move back in with him. We would talk when he picked Jessica up on his visitation days, even spend some time together as a family unit. "It's too hard leaving you and Jessica," he would tell me. "Please move back."

I knew he hadn't changed. I knew he wasn't even capable of changing, and I was not going to move back. But if I had any doubts at all about my decision, David put them to rest. David, who had never supported me. David, the big brother who had never come to my rescue. Knowing that Greg was trying to manipulate me into getting back together, he turned to me one day and said, "If you go back to him, you're going spend your life being treated the way Dad treats Mom. Only worse."

It was an eye-opening comment.

Meanwhile, Greg doubled down, with his manipulation taking another form. "I get too sad having to say goodbye to you and Jessica every week. It's too much for me to take. If you don't come home, I'm going to stop seeing Jessica completely. I'll really have no choice."

It was more than manipulation, and clearly a bluff. Or so I thought. I called him on it. "We're not getting back together," I told him.

Greg held to his word. Because he could not get his way, my daughter would not see her narcissistic father again for the next three and a half years.

Chapter 9

John

I LIVED WITH MY parents for a year. Their controlling ways were mostly in the past; I was an adult and a parent myself, and there wasn't much they could do or say that could affect my life. That didn't stop them from trying to exercise their own authority over Jessica, but overall, they were good with her.

After that year, I found Jessica and me a place of our own—a comfortable bi-level house for rent. Besides teaching and spending time with my daughter, I kept busy with dance lessons at Cheek to Cheek Dance Studio inside the Citadel Theatre downtown. I'd never lost my love of dance, and at Cheek to Cheek, I learned the Argentine tango, the West Coast swing, the salsa, the merengue, the cha-cha, the ballroom waltz, and the rumba. Dancing was something I could immerse myself in.

At a Friday night social after class one time, I met a guy named Chris Jarret. Chris was a male model who, with a pair of brothers, had recently started a modeling and talent agency named Studio 1. Not long after I'd met him, Chris asked if I'd be interested in working as an extra in a movie being shot in Canmore, Alberta. The town was going to be the backdrop for a film titled *Mystery, Alaska*, starring Russell Crowe, Burt Reynolds, Hank Azaria, and a cast of other known and up-and-coming actors. The filmmakers needed about a hundred extras to portray the population of Mystery, a fictional, blue-collar town with a love of hockey. It sounded like a great opportunity to me, and of course I said yes right away.

Working on the film turned out to be a fun adventure, and I learned a lot about how movies are made. When I arrived in Canmore, I checked into the hotel and found Chris, who was giving everyone their call time. It was exciting, with all the extras and production people milling about. The next morning a shuttle bus took us for a short drive to the production site, where I noticed a lot of security, especially around the trailer dressing room areas. It gave me a thrill to think of the actors I might be seeing there. Besides the main stars, Mike Myers was making an appearance in the film. So was Michael McKean, and even Little Richard had a cameo.

Once off the bus, the "wrangler"—the person in charge of looking after the extras—checked us all off and pointed us to the costume department. At one point, a casting agent by the name of Louise Mackiewicz noticed me and asked me my name. Then she said, "Come with me."

We walked over to the lead hairdresser, and Louise asked her if she could make me look like the actress who was playing a reporter in the movie. Then she took my height, weight, and shoe size and checked with wardrobe. The reporter's clothes would fit perfectly. I was more than an extra now. I was a double. I would stand in the actress's place for photo reshoots if she was present in a scene but wasn't available. My pay immediately tripled. The food was better too.

Filming was to be for two weeks, which initially worked out well with my school schedule, but mild weather meant problems with the ice and a need to bring in special snow-making equipment. Everything was delayed. Back in Edmonton, the principal wasn't happy to hear that I needed to extend my absence. Worse, I couldn't give him a firm date of return. Teaching was my primary career, of course, but I didn't want to jeopardize future work with Studio 1 either. Who knows what other opportunities might come my way? In the end, short of finding another permanent special-needs teacher, the principal had no choice but to accommodate my schedule.

Working with celebrity actors was an interesting experience. To us regular folks, some were friendlier than others. Burt Reynolds was a sweetheart of a man, making it a point to talk to everyone each and every day, asking how we were doing, and genuinely interested. Russell Crowe, on the other hand, was more withdrawn and a little less cordial. One day I was talking with a fellow actor, enjoying the extra food and treats and coffees that were available to us, and Crowe came up and angrily accused the other actor of being where he wasn't supposed to be and eating up all the food. Later I was assured that Crowe had only been kidding, but he had that kind of personality where you could never really be sure.

I returned to Edmonton after filming wrapped up, and life returned to normal. But not long after, Lousie Mackiewicz called. She wanted to cast me in a new Canadian–Italian movie called *Almost America*. I was to be a hospital patient who had just given birth. It was another great experience, shorter this time, only one short scene and two evenings of filming. I didn't even have to take time off from teaching. Antonio Frazzi, the director, had a heavy Italian accent, and he gave me my instructions. I was to be in the background talking with another patient on the maternity floor. "You two talk," he told us. "You know, chitchat."

I continued getting the occasional "extra" position, but mostly my life was busy with Jessica, teaching, and the dance classes, which I continued. I rarely dated, both because of lack of time and lack of interest. But without male companionship, I eventually began to feel lonely, especially when Jessica was away. By then Greg had worked his way back into the picture, taking advantage of his visitation rights to try to mend the broken relationship between him and his daughter. It would not be easy. He was spending time with Jessica now, but there was no making up for the fact that he had been absent from her life. He had also remarried, and he and his wife had a baby of their own on the way. All this gave me another reason to wish for a man in my life. I wanted a father figure for Jessica. That figure would never be Greg.

I no longer felt comfortable going to bars and nightclubs to meet someone, so instead, I tried a dating website. It seemed safer and more deliberate. You could read someone's profile and learn something about them before interacting with them. On the site I read the profile of a guy named John, and we seemed to have a lot in common—same tastes in movies, music, and sports. I wrote him a brief message and soon we were exchanging emails. The emails turned into phone calls, and before long we were talking every night.

John—whose legal name was Jean—was the polar opposite of Greg. He was outgoing, charming, and kind. The only problem was that he lived in Calgary, three hours away. Eventually, we decided to meet and I agreed to visit him. We met at a Starbucks in Calgary, and I brought Stephanie with me just in case the meeting didn't go well.

But it did go well. Right from the start, John and I started dating exclusively, with me making trips to Calgary on a weekly basis. I learned that John had been in the Canadian military for twelve years. He'd grown up in Saint-Bruno-de-Montarville, a suburb of Montreal. In 1995 he moved to Alberta, first to Medicine Hat and then Calgary. John was eight years older than me, had never married, and had no children. He'd never been in a long-term relationship. After my experience with Greg, this made me a little wary, but I kept an open mind. After all, John's time in the military had made it hard for him to settle down for a lot of those years.

He'd spent his service mostly in Germany, then later Somalia with the Canadian Airborne Regiment. Somalia was going through both a civil war and a famine, and Canada was there as part of a UN peacekeeping force, sending military personnel in 1992. But the Canadian Airborne Regiment was disbanded in 1995. There had been photo documentation of two Canadian peacekeepers beating a teenager to death. Not only did the beating come to light, but allegations of a cover-up soon followed. The Somalia Affair, as it became known, was one of the most infamous scandals in Canadian military history, creating a huge public outcry and forcing the Minister of National Defence to shutter the Canadian Airborne Regiment. John left the military after that and ended up in Alberta. I hoped his being unattached in the time since was because he simply hadn't found Miss Right yet.

Eventually, I met John's family—his parents, sister, and younger brother, Frank. Frank was dating a woman named Karyn, and the first time I met Karyn was at an upscale restaurant near the hospital where she worked as a nurse. She and Frank were a half hour late for our dinner reservations. It was not a good start, and things got worse. I noticed Karyn seemed cold towards me all through dinner, and at the end of the evening, as we were saying our goodbyes outside the restaurant, she leaned in and said, "I don't know if we'll be seeing each other again, but have a good night." It was a strange ending to an awkward evening.

From that point on, anytime we would see Karyn, she would continue to be aloof around me, and sometimes even hostile. Later I would come to understand that Karyn had struggled with weight issues most of her life. It wasn't hard to figure out that her resentment towards me, and others, was mostly rooted in her own self-image.

John, meanwhile, continued to be the anti-Greg. He liked my friends and never criticized them or tried to keep me from seeing them. He was kind and fun and supportive. A year and a half after we started dating, he asked me to marry him. I said yes and made plans to move to Calgary, even finding a teaching position at a high school. When Greg found out, he went to court to try to stop me, using the same pit bull attorney he'd used before, and accusing me of taking Jessica away from him.

He didn't have much of a case. It was Greg who had left the relationship to begin with, and who had assaulted me, and who had been missing for three and a half years of Jessica's life. I had a fiancé and a job to go to. The best Greg could do was maintain his visitation rights. Once I moved we met in Red Deer, halfway between Calgary and Edmonton, where I would hand over Jessica every other weekend and for the appointed holidays.

When John and I got married, the wedding ceremony was lovely, but the reception was a bit of a debacle—memorable, but for all the wrong reasons. Karyn became so drunk she wiped out on the dance floor. After John and I left for the Westin Hotel that night, she pressed her hand into what remained of our four-tier wedding cake and flattened it. And then she broke some decorations we'd planned on saving as mementos.

John and I settled into marriage, but as time went along, I couldn't help thinking that he was not becoming the father figure I had hoped. He was lukewarm on kids and didn't see himself as a father to Jessica, even after we married and even though Jessica was plainly looking for a father figure. She even wanted to call him Dad, but John wasn't comfortable with that.

"She already has a dad," he would tell me.

"Yes, but you're her stepdad," I would remind him.

In November 2004, John's attitude changed with the birth of our daughter, Jacqueline Marie Liane. When Jacqueline came around, John learned firsthand how special being a parent can be, and as a side result, he became closer to Jessica, becoming more like the father she wanted and needed. It was touching to witness the change that came over him.

Karyn, in the meantime, continued to be Karyn, aloof and resentful. She didn't want anything to do with Jacqueline, one time even refusing to hold her at a family get-together. But it didn't take me long to see that it wasn't just me or my daughters she had issues with. Karyn seemed to dislike everybody equally. I discovered that her being late for dinner the night we met was a passive-aggressive means of control that was a pattern for her with anybody she would set a time to meet with. Everybody talked about it.

And she trusted no one, Frank included. For a little extra money, John and I operated a small vending business, taking care of a few machines for Canadian Blood Services. We went out of town on a short vacation once and arranged for Frank to restock the machines. Frank drove to Canadian Blood Services, telling Karyn beforehand that he had something he needed to do before meeting up with her later. She immediately became suspicious and followed him in her car halfway across town, pulling up behind him in front of Canadian Blood Services, a building surrounded by apartment buildings and condominiums.

She jumped out of her car and marched to the driver's side of Frank's as he was getting out, shouting at him and accusing him of having an affair. "Is this where you meet your mistress?" she demanded to know. "Who is she?"

Frank ran around to the trunk and opened it, showing Karyn all the candy bars, gum, and pop with which he was planning to fill the machines inside the building, telling her that he was helping us out that day. After a while, she was apparently satisfied with his explanation and went home, but her suspicious nature would never go away.

Even so, Frank stayed with Karyn. The general theory that everyone seemed to agree on was that Frank was looking for a mother figure. Karyn, resentful of others, was nurturing to Frank. A wonderful cook and a protective—maybe too protective—force in his life, she compensated for the mother Frank did not have. As it happened, John and Frank's mother had spent most of Frank's life in a mental institution suffering from issues that were exacerbated by her husband's treatment of her. John and Frank's father was emotionally abusive to their mother. There were constant put-downs and tirades, even in front of the kids. Sometimes he was physically abusive. Much later in life John's sister would tell him of the time she witnessed their father holding their mother's head under the dishwater in the kitchen sink.

Two years after our wedding came the wedding of Frank and Karyn. I wasn't invited. Neither was Jessica. I found out from John, who pleaded with his brother to invite us, but Frank, not surprisingly, sided with his fiancée on her decision to exclude us. "It's her day," he told John. "I have to respect her wishes."

It turned out just as well. In the days leading up to the wedding in June 2005, Dad passed away. He'd had heart issues. At one point he'd had a minor heart attack and had spent several days in the hospital. When he returned home, I drove from Calgary to Edmonton to visit my parents every weekend for three weeks. Dad seemed to have recovered and was in good spirits. Before the fourth weekend, Mom told me over the phone that Dad was fine and I didn't need to come every weekend, that maybe I could skip this weekend and come the next. Mom obviously knew best, so I agreed and stayed in Calgary.

Three days later, Dad died. Later I learned that he hadn't felt well during the days leading up to his death. For a long time I was livid with Mom for not sharing that with me, and I felt guilty for not making it home that weekend to see Dad one final time.

The funeral ended up being the same day as Frank and Karyn's wedding, so I couldn't have gone to the wedding even if I had been invited. It had been a beautiful June, but fittingly, on the day of the funeral it rained all day. John attended the service with me and then drove the three hours to Calgary, barely missing his brother's wedding ceremony but getting there in time for the reception.

The marriage, to no one's surprise, would not last. Karyn became increasingly demanding, requiring, among a host of other demands, that Frank be home every evening by six. Everything came to a head on Thanksgiving, just four months after Frank and Karyn were wed. Friends had invited them for an evening Thanksgiving dinner. Frank planned to take part in an afternoon hockey game first, telling Karyn he would meet her at their friend's house afterwards. Karyn didn't like this idea at all. She took Frank's skates and locked them in the guest bedroom, telling him that he had to stay home and that they were going to go to their friends' house together. Frank argued, then caved. For Christmas Karyn bought him a pair of expensive new skates, not as a way to make up for locking his skates away that Thanksgiving but as a clear reminder of that day, a reminder that she was in charge. The skates were symbols of ownership.

To Frank's credit, he finally had enough. In January he asked for a divorce. The marriage didn't last a year. John and I were faring better. At least it seemed that way.

Chapter 10
Disbelieved

AROUND THE TIME OF Karyn and Frank's divorce, I learned something about John that would forever change how I viewed him and how I thought about the strength of our marriage. One time, a childhood friend of John's named Denis was in town for a few days from St. Albert. He was a paramedic and was teaching a CPR class nearby, and John insisted that he stay with us. What I didn't know was that Denis and his wife back in St. Albert were swingers. Moreover, years before, Denis and John had engaged in a threesome with Denis's wife. I'd had no idea. It was something John had never spoken of. I found out from Denis on the second night he'd planned to stay with us.

John was downstairs talking with Patrick, a contractor friend of ours, who was helping us finish the basement. Upstairs, Denis began to flirt with me, saying suggestive things and touching me as he spoke. Patrick had come upstairs a couple of times for tools and took notice.

"John," he told him in the basement, "I think your buddy is coming on to your wife."

John came up and saw Denis talking to me. "So, what's going on?" John asked casually.

"Oh, not much." Denis smiled. "Lori and I are just chatting about this and that."

I took John's hand and led him into the kitchen, where I told him Denis was acting inappropriately.

"Oh, honey," John said, "I'm sure it's just your imagination. He wouldn't do anything like that, okay? He's an old friend of mine. Now, I've got to get back downstairs."

John left, apparently satisfied, and Denis continued to flirt. I became furious, grabbed my car keys, and headed for the garage. Denis followed, jumping into the passenger seat before I could back the car out.

"Hey, you shouldn't be driving when you're upset," he said. "We should talk about this." Then Denis explained to me about the swinging, about the history he and John had, and that he and John had talked about a threesome with me.

My mouth fell open. "I don't believe it," I said.

"It's all true."

"So John is okay with all this? A threesome?!"

"Yes. He said it was up to you. So what do you think?"

And then, before I could say a word, Denis took my hand and jammed it down his pants. I could feel his growing penis. I jerked my hand away, fled from the car, and ran down to the basement to tell John what had happened.

John was incredulous. "He did what?!"

"And not only that," I said, trying to catch my breath. "He said you wanted us to have a threesome. He said you'd planned this all along! My God, John, is that true?"

I was expecting a denial, but John hesitated. Finally he said, "Look, I don't do that stuff anymore. I told Denis that. And I also told him you wouldn't be into it anyway. He shouldn't have said anything."

I was seething.

"Okay, listen, I'll go talk to him," John said, and then he went to find Denis. He came back down to the basement ten minutes later.

"I'm sorry, Lori, but Denis said he didn't do anything."

"What? And you believe him?"

"Well, I mean, what do you want me to say? He's a longtime friend from way back. We practically grew up together. I have to believe him, don't I?"

"But I'm your wife."

"I know, and I hate to see you upset. Denis apologizes for any misunderstanding but swears he didn't do anything. I've got to take him at his word, you know? But listen, both of us felt it might be awkward if he stayed here tonight, so he's calling a cab and going to a hotel. Okay?"

Nothing was okay. "You don't believe me," I said.

John shrugged. "I'm sorry, but . . . he's my friend."

Our marriage would never be the same.

From that day on, John would swear that Denis had never lied to him. "We have no secrets," he would tell me. I knew better. It was Denis who had told me about the emotional abuse John's father had leveled at John's mother. As his best childhood friend, it was not uncommon for Denis to hang out at John's house, even when John was out somewhere, and he'd seen firsthand the insults and mistreatment, incidents that he'd never shared with John, incidents John hadn't seen. Denis had secrets.

As far as I was concerned, all that was beside the point. I was John's wife. And his confidence in Denis's word meant more than just believing Denis. It meant he didn't believe *me*. Without using the word, he was calling me a liar, implying that I had made up Denis's assault in the garage. And why would I have done so anyway? Why would I have made such a thing up? When I would ask him, he'd have no good answer, mumbling only about "misunderstanding," as if a person could misunderstand having their hand jammed down the front of someone's pants.

All of that was in addition to John giving permission to Denis to ask me in the first place if I'd want to engage in a threesome.

As with the rape, I found myself traumatized twice—first by the actions of Denis and then the inaction of my husband. Except that in at least one way, this might have been worse. At least my parents believed me about the rape.

I felt abandoned, and I found myself wondering if the marriage was a mistake. I tried to put the thought out of my head.

I had to. I was pregnant.

It should have been a wonderful time for us, but the marriage was suffering. And the stress took a toll on my health. The pregnancy was a difficult one. With Jessica and Jacqueline, things had been easy. This time I was constantly nauseous and felt drained of energy. Towards the end of the pregnancy, I developed gestational diabetes. It didn't help that our baby was overdue. Two weeks past my due date, my ob-gyn planned for me to be induced the following Monday. The baby, however, as babies often do, decided to take charge of the scheduling and came naturally that Sunday morning.

Like the pregnancy itself, the birth was very different from my first two. Even my treatment by the nurses was different. Before my ob-gyn arrived at the hospital, I was looked after by a nurse who asked if this was my first baby. I told her it was my third, and she said, "Oh, you're a breeder."

Strange comments aside, my beautiful, healthy baby boy, all eight pounds of him, was born on a sunny, warm day—September 17, 2006.

I had wanted to name him Braedon, but John disliked the name. He preferred Michael. Although I liked Michael, I thought it was too common. Besides, we already had two Michaels on Braedon's side of the family, a cousin and a brother-in-law. A name we both agreed we liked was Johnathan, but with the non-traditional spelling.

Johnathan Joseph Markus Rheault was my first baby to sleep through the night, something my daughters didn't master until their second year. In fact, JR, as he would affectionately be called, could at times be so difficult to wake up that I would need to pour water on him. Even undressing him would not wake him, making for some alarming moments.

Johnathan's arrival did little to mend the tear in our relationship. John would never take my side in the Denis incident and, instead, turned things around and accused me of having trust issues. Over the months, and then years, we continued to drift farther apart but stayed together because of the kids. John, with his own childhood in mind, was determined not to have the children become products of a broken home. I went along with it, recognizing the importance to my children of having their father in their lives.

Three times along the way we tried marital counseling. The first two times John stopped going when the counselors sided with me. Both said almost the same thing: "John, she's your wife. You really need to believe her and take her side. That's what marriage is about. This goes beyond the incident with your friend. This is about supporting the woman you married."

The third counselor was a woman who didn't comment specifically on the Denis incident but who seemed more inclined to back John's assessment of me and our marriage and my "trust" issues. She would pick apart what I would say, and more than once I noticed she would lean in to say something to us while putting her hand on John's knee. That was the end of our try at marriage counseling.

From there, John and I more or less shared the house while living different lives. He'd take Johnathan to hockey practice; I'd take Jacqueline to soccer. We'd both go to work each day, seeing each other briefly in the morning and then again at night. We would do family things together but rarely do anything as a couple. It was a marriage in name only.

Naturally, we developed separate interests, and one of mine was running. It started as a five-kilometer charity run that Jessica and I signed up for in 2010. She was seventeen by then, and the run was for children with special needs, a cause near and dear to my heart. It was a hot June day, but I was enamored by the cheering crowd and the support and encouragement of the spectators and the other runners. I'd had no intention of pursuing running as a hobby, but Running Room, a shoe and sportswear chain, sponsored free running clubs, and right after the race, I joined one. They also had training programs you could join for a fee, and I joined the 5K program.

I ran some more 5K races and then decided I wanted to push myself a little harder. I signed up for their 10K program. Not long after that, I signed up for their half-marathon and then their marathon program. The training was invaluable and the meetings were fun. I made friends that I have to this day. We ran marathons in Calgary and Edmonton, but also in Victoria, and even Oregon and Chicago. For the Chicago Marathon, not just anyone could enter. You had to apply and provide documentation that you'd run a recent marathon under a certain time. It felt good to be able to qualify. I felt like a seasoned pro.

I loved running. I knew it was good for my physical well-being, but I noticed it helped my mental well-being too. Enormously. I found myself far less stressed and anxious. And completing the marathons gave me a profound sense of accomplishment, not just for finishing but for having done all the work leading up to each race—the training, the setting of goals, the need to be accountable for my progress. I was proud of myself. The runs were all for charity, which I took seriously, diligently getting donations from friends and family, all for a higher cause.

Back home John and I continued to live separate lives. For this, maybe there was enough blame to go around. The fact is, I did have trust issues. My life had not been without betrayals, starting with the sexual assault by a friend of the family, which was bad enough, and then my parents doing nothing about it. My childhood was filled with reasons for me not to trust. There was the wide discrepancy between how I was treated and how David was treated. There were the cats my parents took to the SPCA, lying to me that the cats had run away. There were the kids at Hardisty who treated me with such contempt. There were the incidents when only by the grace of God I was able to escape potential rape, kidnapping, or worse by men who had followed me in the streets. There were the men who'd hit on me—a young teenager—while walking alone to McCauley Junior High. There was Cindy, who feigned friendship so that she could rifle through the coat pockets of my father for money to steal. And there was Greg, who repaid my love with verbal and physical abuse.

It was not easy for me to trust.

But of course that's what made the Denis incident so significant and heartbreaking to me. I'd been willing to try. I swept my past aside and put my faith into my marriage. I'd met the man I had wanted to spend the rest of my life with—a friend, a partner, a confidante. We were going to have a child together. Then, one night, an old friend of his assaulted me and later denied it. My husband, my confidante, chose to believe him and not me.

As the kids grew, John and I both felt that the best years of our lives were slipping by. Both of us wanted to find love again, which meant we needed to move on from each other, despite the effects it might have on the kids. A loveless home was perhaps worse. I felt the need to move on more than John did, at least initially. When we finally had divorce papers written up, John hesitated to sign them, and after signing them, he stayed in our home for a time, living in the basement until he could find a suitable condo. Eventually he moved out.

I should have felt liberated, but I felt sad and wounded. My marriage had failed. And although it hadn't been good, John and I had stayed together so long that being single again was strange. I grieved for the marriage that might have been but never was, the divorce making it official. I knew that it would take quite some time for me to heal.

Chapter 11
#MeToo

I KEPT UP MY running, which continued to provide its own kind of therapy. So did raising my kids. I became determined to give them a better childhood than what I had. They would have the unconditional love and support I never received. I wanted them to feel safe and secure. I wanted them to feel *heard*, the one thing I never felt growing up.

I have few photographs of myself as a child, but when I look at them, they bring tears to my eyes. My heart melts as I look at the little girl in the pictures—so innocent and naïve. I think of all the things she doesn't know, the experiences that will shape her. She doesn't know the pain she will feel and the struggles with self-doubt, self-worth, and self-acceptance. Nor is she aware of the walls she will build around her heart, walls that will feel like mountain-sized boulders she'll have to spend years chiseling through simply to feel enough space to live and breathe. She has no idea how much she'll isolate herself from everyone, most painfully from herself. How she'll feel so alone. How she'll feel that no matter what she achieves, it will never be good enough. That *she* will never be good enough.

My children would have different lives, and I worked to instill in them a sense of self-worth, the self-worth that remained out of reach for me. They'd never have to feel alone or unaccepted or unloved.

Besides raising my children and running, I became involved in some more TV projects. These were always interesting, each unique in its own way. I found a new agent in Calgary, who found me a job as a stand-in on *Joe Pickett*, a neo-Western crime drama set in Wyoming but with a lot of the filming taking place south of Calgary in High River. The series was produced by Paramount Television and ran for two seasons. My job as a stand-in was to take the place of an actor and run through a scene while the director and crew made sure the lighting was just right, there were no problematic reflections, the cameras were in the right places, and that everything else was all set so that the starring actors could swoop in afterwards and do the scene without anything on the set needing to be changed or adjusted. It's kind of a dry run for the film crew.

It was interesting work. I enjoyed being part of the "Second Team." The director would call out, "Okay, Second Team, you're up!" It was also very cool to be working next to the main actors on the show, to watch them deliver their lines, and to try to emulate them. But we stand-ins worked long days. The main cast members had all the fun, but we had to repeat scenes over and over. We had to get to the set early in the morning, where we'd get our lines for the scenes each day. I played the stand-in for actress Sharon Lawrence, but I was also the stand-in for several parts, making for a full day that often didn't wrap up until the evening. Worse, I was driving to High River each day from the other side of Calgary. By the time I got home each night, it was all I could do to make myself a little dinner and flop into bed.

It was on the set of *Joe Pickett* where I first encountered the sexual harassment that had, by then, become such a glaring issue in the entertainment industry. A guest star was on the set one morning, and we were running through a scene. Some changes were made to the script, and we had to do the scene over a few times. At the end of one of the run-throughs, maybe in what he thought was a playful way, the actor slapped me hard on the butt and then put his arm around me. This elicited laughter from all the men on the set but none of the women. We finished the scene with the director smiling and telling us how well we'd done.

One of the assistant directors, a woman, came up to me and said, "Lori, are you all right? I heard the slap from clear across the room." The concern she showed me in that moment, checking on me in front of the crew and other actors, was something I never forgot. Later she talked to the guest star, who came to me and apologized for getting, as he told me, "carried away."

But the matter didn't end there. That evening my agent called to check in, as she normally did at the end of each day, and I told her what had happened on the set. In turn, she talked to the person who was in charge of the extras, who then talked to one of the executive producers. In no time Paramount opened an investigation during which everyone was questioned about the incident. I'll never know if it was just a coincidence, but the guest actor was written out of the script after only three episodes.

On one hand, it felt good to know that such behavior was so quickly dealt with. It was surprising, in fact. I knew that only a few years before, nobody would have done a thing. Circumstances were different now. On the other hand, I couldn't forget the laughter of the men on the set that day. It took another woman on the set to understand my distress. And my agent was a woman, and the executive producer happened to be a woman too. Would an investigation have taken place had my agent or the executive producer been men? Yes, the #MeToo movement was in full swing by then, but were men even getting the message? More cynically, I wondered if the Paramount investigation had more to do with wanting to avoid the bad publicity that could come from a sexual harassment allegation than from wanting to do the right thing.

I remembered the start of the widespread #MeToo movement, especially in the entertainment field. In October 2017, *The New York Times* published an article detailing their investigation of Hollywood producer Harvey Weinstein. Weinstein had been a powerful and successful producer, having won Academy, Emmy, and BAFTA Awards, and more. He was perhaps best known for producing *Shakespeare in Love*, which won the Oscar for Best Picture in 1999. But the *Times* uncovered allegations of sexual harassment stretching over three decades. More than a dozen women had accused Weinstein of harassment, assault, and rape.

The initial upshot was that Weinstein was dismissed from his production company, bounced out of the Academy of Motion Picture Arts and Sciences, and expelled from other industry trade groups. In time, criminal charges would be brought against him in both Los Angeles and New York, and Weinstein would go to jail. As of this writing, he's in New York's Rikers Island prison.

But the larger ramifications came from the groundswell of activism that erupted from the Weinstein case. After the *Times* article, actress Alyssa Milano posted a message on Twitter saying, "If all the women who have been sexually harassed or assaulted wrote 'Me too' as a status, we might give people a sense of the magnitude of the problem." A lot of high-profile actresses took her up on it, including Uma Thurman, Ashley Judd, Jennifer Lawrence, and Gwyneth Paltrow, who won a Best Actress Academy Award for Weinstein's *Shakespeare in Love*. Soon other actresses, as well as women in other fields, posted #MeToo. Hundreds followed, then thousands, then millions, turning #MeToo into a household expression.

Interestingly, the phrase had been around since at least 2006. Milano got the idea from a social media post back then from activist and community organizer Tarana Burke, a victim herself of sexual assault and rape as a child. A thirteen-year-old girl confided to Burke one day that she had been sexually assaulted. Burke had been at a loss for words and later wished she had simply said, "Me too." When Milano used the same words in her Tweet, a movement was born.

But was it getting anywhere? I found out later that in the investigation of the *Joe Pickett* incident, the male members of the set as well as the director tried to downplay it. Fortunately, the cameras had been rolling and everything was on tape. Otherwise, I can't help thinking that the downplaying would have taken the form of outright denial.

Nonetheless, I tried not to let the incident sour me on the business, which I still found enjoyable. After finding me work on *Joe Pickett*, my agent got me a stint on *Heartland*, a long-running family comedy-drama set on a ranch in Alberta. This time I was an extra—an actor in the background of a crowd scene, or maybe a ranch hand walking by. I liked it. Being an extra was much less demanding than being a stand-in. It didn't pay as well, but I didn't have to work every day and the days weren't nearly as long.

I didn't experience or witness any sexual harassment on the set of *Heartland*, but that didn't mean everyone was an angel. There are actors who feel entitled, and that entitlement often takes the form of rudeness and insensitivity. I watched one of the main cast members regularly lose it on others, often yelling at the director and other people on the set. He chastised me one time for "blocking his light." But the rest of the cast was nice, and I did my best to put my head down and do my job each day.

Heartland was followed by a short stint on *My Life with the Walter Boys*, a ten-episode teen drama. I was an extra in a scene that was filmed at the Jubilee Auditorium in the north part of Calgary, not far from where I lived. I became an extra, as well, in a popular miniseries titled *Under the Banner of Heaven*, a true crime drama set in Utah and filmed in Calgary that starred Andrew Garfield and Daisy Edgar-Jones. I wound up in a photo with the main cast members that was printed in a story in *The Los Angeles Times*. I also had an opportunity to work on a short film.

Each project was interesting in its own way, but of course some of the glamour of the entertainment industry fades when you work in it. Seeing the end result on a screen doesn't quite cover everything that goes into filming a movie or TV episode—the hard work, the long hours, the retakes, and naturally, the personalities one has to interact with, some nice, some not so nice.

And some predatory.

The #MeToo movement continues, of course. From the entertainment field, it moved into the sports industry, broadcasting, politics, and eventually into the general workplace. But there is a long way to go. According to Statistics Canada, one in four women in Canada have experienced inappropriate sexual behaviours in the workplace. One in three women have experienced unwanted sexual behaviour in public. One in seventeen have been, at some point in their lives, raped. Numbers are similar throughout the US and Europe too. And as long as you have a culture in which men stand around and laugh at unwanted sexual contact, the numbers won't get any better.

Chapter 12
To the Top of the Hill

What I've learned in adulthood is that sexual abuse and sexual predation is, sadly, commonplace. The #MeToo movement has certainly revealed this, and I have seen it firsthand. I am probably more conscious of it because of my own experience, going back to age ten. My radar is especially sensitive to victimization and, of course, that's one of the lingering effects of childhood trauma.

Some statistics: According to the Survey of Safety in Public and Private Spaces (SSPPS), conducted by the Canadian Research Data Centre Network, three in ten Canadians have experienced childhood victimization, meaning at least one instance of physical or sexual abuse by an adult before the age of fifteen. Sexual abuse itself, though less prevalent than strictly physical abuse, was still reported by 7.8 percent of survey respondents. If 7.8 percent doesn't sound like a lot, consider this: Based on population, 7.8 percent means over *three million* Canadians have been sexually abused as children.

Per capita numbers are similar in the United States and throughout the world, with some countries being worse than others. The SSPPS survey noted that the likelihood of negative adult outcomes, including poor mental and physical health, drug and alcohol use, and subsequent victimization in adulthood, were higher among those with a history of childhood victimization, thus making childhood victimization a significant public health issue. The National Society for the Prevention of Cruelty to Children (NSPCC), the leading children's charity in the United Kingdom, backs this up, adding that adults who were abused as children often find it "hard to cope with life's stresses, get a good job, or be a good parent."

Here's the worst part, and the part I know all too well: According to the SSPPS survey, only 7.7 percent of abuse incidents are reported to police or child protection services. Naturally, to a large degree, this is often a function of the victim's inaction. According to the NSPCC, the reasons for a child not disclosing an abusive incident, even to a trusted parent, include "having no one to turn to, not understanding they were being abused, being ashamed or embarrassed, being afraid of the consequences of speaking out."

In my case, I spoke out. I told my parents. But that's where the reporting ended. My parents failed to take any further steps for some of the same reasons children fail to take further steps: shame, embarrassment, fear of consequences. Except that my parents were not children. They were grown adults. What they didn't understand at the time was that, although the consequences they feared never came to pass (the idea that they might be somehow blamed), other consequences *did* come to pass. I was left feeling twice victimized, first by Fred and then by my own mother and father, who could have taken action but didn't.

This would have repercussions for me my entire life, repercussions that went above and beyond the rape itself. If you're a parent or a responsible adult, there is never an excuse to not report childhood abuse. It's stunning now to imagine my parents essentially looking the other way after learning that their ten-year-old daughter had been raped. In fact, it's more than stunning. As a parent myself, I find it unimaginable.

And the reason my parents looked the other way—this is what made it so bad. They didn't fail to report the rape for my benefit, but for theirs. It was wrong either way, but if I thought for a moment that their decision to keep things quiet was to somehow help me, to shield me from having to relive the incident or to keep me safe from any unwanted attention it might have drawn, maybe I could have lived with that. It would have been the wrong decision, but at least it might have been made with good intentions. I could probably even convince myself they made it out of love. But I knew better: My parents decided to quash the incident to save themselves from embarrassment. They didn't want to be victims themselves.

Of course, for me, the effects include trust issues—that sensitive radar. But there were other effects from my childhood. Like my perfectionism, rooted in my parents' emotional abuse. Besides the obvious favoritism towards David, there were the constant belittling comments. "We had you only to take care of us in our old age" still rings in my head.

If there weren't the comments, there was silence. I felt ignored and unseen. For two years I begged my parents to take me out of a school where I was constantly bullied and belittled, and for two years they did nothing. What it all led to, what it would lead to for any child, was an ongoing need for approval, approval that I would never receive. This need for approval, coupled with an exaggerated need for control (typical for trauma victims), made some degree of perfectionism a foregone conclusion.

It has also led to a life of people-pleasing behavior, or at least a strong disinclination to want to speak up for myself, even when the circumstances warrant speaking up. I've never been a large person, and I've always managed to maintain a healthy weight. But several years ago, through weight-training that I'd incorporated into my fitness regime, I gained eight pounds. A group of runners who knew me made comments about how I looked better, that before, I looked "skinny and gaunt and unhealthy." They were sure I'd been on some "crazy fad diet." I tried to explain that my diet had remained pretty much the same. I'd always been at a healthy weight. But the words were met with skepticism and my voice trailed off. I wanted to argue. I wanted to tell them that remarks about how I looked and conjectures about what I ate were off-limits. Who tells someone that they used to look "skinny and gaunt and unhealthy"? And why? I couldn't argue. With my need for approval, I couldn't bring myself to confront their insensitivity. Instead, I felt relieved when the conversation went in another direction.

There have been other times when people made disrespectful, even humiliating comments, and my reaction was not to challenge them as I should have but to try, instead, to fight back the tears I found forming in my eyes. Trauma can do that to a person. Trauma can bring about strong emotions, leaving you paralyzed and overwhelmed.

That's me, anyway. For others the effects of early trauma manifest themselves in some of the ways described by the SSPPS and NSPCC above—poor mental and physical health, drug and alcohol use, and so on. The hope, of course, is that victims will, at some point, realize that life can surely be better. That's what happened with me. I decided I no longer wanted to suffer from the effects I was experiencing from my own childhood trauma. I wanted healing. I wanted to move forward.

When I ultimately reached that point, I finally sought help.

But seeking help, I discovered, isn't exactly a straight road. I started with BounceBack, a free program from the Canadian Mental Health Association supposedly designed to help adults with depression or anxiety. You're given workbooks, each with different subjects like "Understanding Low Mood and Depression" and "Facing Fears and Overcoming Avoidance," and assigned a coach to support and encourage you. The problem is that your interaction with the coach is only ten to fifteen minutes every two to three weeks. My coach became angry with me for working on what he felt was the wrong workbook. The workbooks were online, and I downloaded the one I was most interested in, the one I was certain would be the most helpful. In fact, the program stipulated that you could design your own program. Apparently, after a ten-minute interview three weeks before, my coach knew better than I did about what program I should be pursuing. I dared to disagree, and it was pretty clear to me that he didn't like having his authority challenged. "I don't think this program is for you," he said testily before hanging up. I couldn't help but wonder if maybe there was a workbook for him.

My second attempt at getting help was through CASA Mental Health, a nonprofit organization partnered with the University of Alberta and Alberta Health Services. This was more promising. Zoom sessions were an hour with a counselor skilled specifically in sexual assault. Unfortunately, my counselor didn't quite know what to do with me. She offered breathing exercises, even though I was not necessarily feeling anxious or stressed. My trust issues, for example, were deep-seated and subtle. Yes, they produced anxiety, but only during certain interactions with others, causing me not to go into panic mode but rather to feel a sort of lingering misapprehension about people in general. The bigger context was that these feelings were affecting my quality of life. I tried to explain all this while my counselor googled around the internet for ways that I might be helped, something I could obviously do on my own.

Finally, I found a private psychologist who was a tremendous help, thus affirming the adage that you get what you pay for. In our first session we talked about the rape and about my parents' reaction. I told her about the trip to Trinidad and Tobago. I told her that, back when I was lost to my principal and those who had sent me on the trip, there was a part of me that believed my parents had something to do with it, that it was intentional. It was only later, when I saw the anger my parents showed at discovering that nobody had a clue as to where I'd been, that I realized for certain that they were not trying to get rid of me. But the fact that I'd initially harbored those suspicions spoke volumes.

The sessions continued from there. One goal became learning how to look objectively at situations and people, to avoid looking through the prism of mistrust that I had essentially been saddled with in childhood. After all, there had been times when my misapprehensions had been affirmed—like the time my friend Melody and I had been followed by the two men or the time I had seen the man waiting for me on the bike path by the river. In both cases my fears were spot on. A sensitive radar doesn't necessarily mean an inaccurate one. But it becomes problematic if mistrust is the default setting. Regarding everything with suspicion can be a heavy, exhausting burden. How do I know when my intuitions are accurate, and how do I know when they are being misinformed by my own baggage?

Another goal of the therapy was to try to stop all the perfectionism and people pleasing. I don't have to be perfect. I don't need to control everything. And I surely don't need to let people get away with hurtful, rude, insensitive comments or behaviors. I can speak up. I can say something.

I have worth.

One major focus of the therapy was to try to reconcile in my mind my parents' action—or more precisely, inaction—to get a better understanding of where their heads were at. How did they arrive at the choices they made? What life events of their own pasts informed their decision? Why did they do nothing about the rape? Why did they allow me to be bullied and harassed at school? I've tried to make excuses for them, but the excuses fall flat. "It was just their generation," I've often told myself. But it wasn't. I've met other victims of childhood trauma my age whose parents supported them, who did the right things at the right time.

But I know that at some point I need to let it all go, to find some way to forgive them. To move beyond it all. Unfortunately, the time to address my parents' decision personally—face to face—has slipped by. Both have passed away. Dad, of course, died in 2005, just days after Mom had assured me he was fine, keeping me from seeing him one last time. Mom passed away ten years later—March 2015. She died on the day of their wedding anniversary.

Mom had been in pain for a while. She'd always told us she had "soft" bones, prone to occasional aches and pains. But then, in early 2015, the pain became steady and intense. David took her to the doctor, who diagnosed her with arthritis. In the end it was something much more insidious. Mom had bladder cancer, and it had spread. She died just a few months later. Towards the end, with Mom lying in her hospital bed in pain, a nurse turned to David and me and said, "That's what happens when you smoke." This was the second time in my life a nurse made a cold, insensitive comment. I still remembered the time a nurse had lectured me about my suicide attempt. "You should be ashamed of yourself, young lady," she had said to me.

This time I was just as floored, just as speechless. I hadn't yet reached a point where I could bring myself to fire back, but David spoke up. "My mother has never smoked a day in her life," he seethed. It was true. She was always adamantly opposed to smoking. The nurse shrugged and left the room.

With Mom and Dad both gone, I had lost the chance to confront them about their inaction after the rape, their inaction with the bullying I sustained at Hardisty, and their general lack of interest in me as a child. I had lost the chance to get them to understand the long-term effects of feeling unheard and unloved.

And I had lost the chance to understand *them*. Maybe forgive them. The last time I had expressed my feelings—truly expressed them—was the time I had exploded on them at the age of eighteen. The time I had I lost it and screamed my frustrations at them.

Ten years have come and gone since my mother's death. In that time, a lot has changed. I have grown in important ways. I am learning to trust. I am learning to let go of circumstances outside of my control. I am learning to speak up.

I have a wonderful man in my life now, and for the very first time, I know what it means to be loved and accepted and cared for. I've had the unconditional love of my children, of course, but for a person to want to seek me out, to spend their life with me, to support and understand me—this is all new. In truth, I never knew this kind of love existed. I had never felt it, even though it's clear to me now that my soul has always been seeking it.

But I am a work in progress. Not a day goes by that I don't think about—for no rational reason—losing this love. In the world of psychology, this is known as catastrophic thinking or *catastrophizing*. It's fearing the worst possible outcome. Hypothetical worst-case scenarios plague my thoughts. My therapist tells me it's my mind's way of anticipating and protecting myself against pain. It's both a manifestation of my anxiety and a cause of it, keeping me in a loop of negative thoughts and fears. It's not a feeling that bad things may happen; it's a feeling that bad things *will* happen. The scenarios seem to me like premonitions of a very real, inescapable future.

The upshot is that I have trouble trusting, trouble opening up, trouble being vulnerable. Joe's been patient, but I have not been easy to be with at times. I push him away, often without even realizing it. The key for me is to recognize the scenarios for what they are: imaginings rooted in my own past, and not the reality of my life today. I'm getting better at shifting my thoughts away from the dark road they take me down. Before, I could not recognize what was happening in my head and my fears would become obsessions, and it would be a monumental task to turn away from them. I'm learning now to stop the scenarios before they spin out of my control, to replace the dark thoughts with positive ones.

It's not easy. Too many mornings I wake up feeling like a deflated balloon. I admire those people who seem to face life's daily trials with positivity and hope. Those are my role models. I know that somewhere within me, I have the potential to be like them. Anyone can. But it's a battle. Some days it's a long run up a steep hill, but I have certainly done that before. Life, I have come to believe, is a lot like distance running. To be successful at it, you need to train. You need to be determined. You need to be consistent, and you need to have patience.

I'll get there. Of that I am sure. I'll reach the top of that hill. When that happens, I'll spend a moment taking in the view. And then I'll turn on my heels and keep going.

Epilogue

Writing this book was daunting. It required me to own my story. To be brutally honest. To be vulnerable. To revisit the most difficult parts of my life. And the idea of actually *sharing* my story—this was, and continues to be, even more daunting. The whole process has been mentally, emotionally, and physically draining.

But to achieve healing and inner peace, I determined that it was necessary to embrace my past—to name the hurt and face it. Throughout the writing process, I grieved as the unwanted memories of my trials came flooding back. Quite often I would get severe headaches that would sometimes last a couple of days.

It hurts going back in time and remembering the longing to feel loved by those who withheld it. For years I could not forgive my parents for not being attuned and responsive in my formative years, for being cold and unloving. Yet it's been so long since their passing, and I do miss my mother and father dearly. I suppose I'll always have to live with some level of ambivalence towards them.

I find the pain and the vulnerability mitigated by the thought that my story in some way might resonate with someone going through something similar. I know from experience that support and understanding are in short supply, even from friends who claim to support you but then waver and pull away if you open up to them about the depth of your depression. I once heard Oprah Winfrey put it like this: Lots of people want to ride with you in the limo, but what you want is someone who will take the bus with you when the limo breaks down.

Just know that there are others like you who have suffered and are suffering. And know that you are never alone.

I have received much comfort from the words of Matthew 28:20: "Lo, I am with you always, even unto the end of the world." In my weakest moments, I have been reminded of 2 Corinthians 12:9: "My grace is sufficient for thee: for my strength is made perfect in weakness. Most gladly therefore will I rather glory in my infirmities, that the power of Christ may rest upon me."

I do know that God answers prayers. I have personally experienced how God has transformed someone's heart from a cold one and softened it. And God has given me signs that he wants me to continue living. God has been with me in times of danger. Earlier in the book, I wondered where God was during the rape. In the course of writing this book, I have come to believe that God is never not there. God is always present. If we can't see or hear God, it is because we have not learned how to look or how to listen. Looking back, I do not believe, when I was only ten years old, that I had the spiritual capacity or maturity to sense God in that moment. But God was there, suffering right alongside me.

God knows. God understands.

If you are suffering, know that you are not meant to. This is not what the universe wants for you. Seek help. There is a list of resources that follows this epilogue.

Don't be afraid to reach out and find the help and support that you deserve.
—LL

For Help

In Canada

The Ending Violence Association of Canada. A national nonprofit organization that works collaboratively with its member organizations and others to provide a unified, pan-Canadian voice on the issue of sexual violence. Has lists of sexual assault centres, crisis lines, support services, shelters, and other resources by province. https://endingviolencecanada.org/getting-help/.

988 Lifeline. 24/7/365 suicide and crisis hotline. Counselors available by simply dialing 988. https://988lifeline.org/. (Also available in the United States.)

In the United States

RAINN (Rape, Abuse & Incest National Network). Nation's largest anti–sexual violence organization. RAINN created and operates the National Sexual Assault Hotline. 800.656.HOPE (4673). https://rainn.org/.

National Domestic Violence Hotline. Available 24/7/365, providing essential tools and support to help survivors of domestic violence so they can live their lives free of abuse. 1.800.799.SAFE (7233), or text START to 88788. https://www.thehotline.org/.

Crisis Text Line. Free, 24/7, high-quality text-based mental health support and crisis intervention. For help, simply text HOME to 741741.

In the United States and Canada

The Trauma Foundation. Supporting the healing of unresolved trauma for individuals, families, and communities. www.thetraumafoundation.org.

Acknowledgements

I would like to recognize and express gratitude for God's role in providing guidance, wisdom, and blessings throughout my journey.

I want to thank everyone who ever said a kind word or anything positive to me. I heard it all, and it meant something.

I wish to express gratitude to my three children—Jessica, Jacqueline, and Johnathan (J.R.). I am supremely proud and honoured to be your mom. You will forever be my greatest joys and accomplishments. I love you.

A special thank you to my partner, Joe, who is a constant source of support and inspiration. You are my person, my confidante, my love, and my best friend. I am forever grateful for your love and belief in me.

Many thanks to my editor, Jerry Payne, for his professionalism and belief in this book.

And, finally, my blessings go out to every reader who finds a "piece" of themselves within these chapters.

www.ingramcontent.com/pod-product-compliance
Lightning Source LLC
Chambersburg PA
CBHW030439010526
44118CB00011B/708